DAVID WEATHERLY
LONE STAR STATE MONSTERS:
CRYPTIDS & LEGENDS
OF
TEXAS
FOREWORD BY NICK REDFERN

Eerie Lights Publishing
Eerielights.com
Eerielightspublishing.com

DAVID WEATHERLY
LONE STAR STATE MONSTERS:
CRYPTIDS & LEGENDS
OF
TEXAS
FOREWORD BY NICK REDFERN

Based on interviews and research conducted by David Weatherly

ISBN: 978-1-945950-42-1 (Paperback)

Published by:

EERIE LIGHTS
Eerie Lights Publishing
Eerielights.com
Eerielightspublishing.com

Cover art by Mister Sam Shearon
MisterSamShearon.com

Editor: Jerry Hajewski

Book layout/design: SMAK
smakgraphics.com

Printed in the United States of America

Also by David Weatherly

Strange Intruders
Eerie Companions: A History of Haunted Dolls
Black Eyed Children

The Monsters of America Series
Silver State Monsters: Cryptids & Legends of Nevada
Copper State Monsters: Cryptids & Legends of Arizona
Monsters of the Last Frontier: Cryptids & Legends of Alaska
Monsters at the Crossroads: Cryptids & Legends of Indiana
Monsters of the Tar Heel State: Cryptids & Legends of North Carolina
Peach State Monsters: Cryptids & Legends of Georgia
Monsters of Big Sky Country: Cryptids & Legends of Montana
Palmetto State Monsters: Cryptids & Legends of South Carolina
Beehive State Monsters: Cryptids & Legends of Utah
Monsters of the Hawkeye State: Cryptids & Legends of Iowa
Monsters of the Green Mountain State: Cryptids & Legends of Vermont
Sunshine State Monsters: Cryptids & Legends of Florida
Monsters of the Pine Tree State: Cryptids & Legends of Maine

The Haunted Series (co-authored with Ross Allison)
Haunted Toys
Haunted Ships & Lighthouses
Haunted Churches
Haunted Prisons
Haunted Historic Hotels of the Pacific Coast

Shadow Chaser (co-authored with Sean Austin)
Shadow Chaser: The In-Between (co-authored with Sean Austin)

Wood Knocks: A Journal of Sasquatch Research
Volume One
Volume Two
Volume Three
Volume Four
Volume Five

Table of Contents

PART FOUR:
STRANGE BEASTS
AND CURIOUS LEGENDS

LONE STAR STATE MONSTERS by David Weatherly

Foreword

I was very pleased when David Weatherly asked me to write a foreword for the latest of his Monsters of America series. The reason being that although I was born in the U.K., I moved to live in the United States twenty-four years ago. My destination was Texas. I love the Lone Star State, with its variations of deep forests, flatlands, and the wild animals, many I'd never seen before—aside from on a television screen. So, you can see how and why this particular edition of the series is a really significant one for me. With that said, let's get to the heart of this book: the monsters and strange creatures of Texas.

The first Texas cryptid I heard of was the Goat Man. It was a creature that caused a lot of chaos back in 1969. Actually, it didn't take me long to know that the U.S. has quite a lot of Goat Men. Texas has several itself including the creature at White Rock Lake, the monster of Denton's Goatman Bridge, and another beast that prowled around on Greer Island. Hoofed, furry, and sometimes fishy no less. Real monsters indeed!

Is Bigfoot present in Texas? Most people think of the Bigfoot creatures dwelling in the deep forests of the Pacific Northwest but there have been Bigfoot sightings reported from all over Texas. Take for instance, Ray Roberts Lake State Park. The park has an impressive 29,350 acres so there's plenty of room for the hairy creature to roam about and there have been several reports from the area. On several occasions, I have seen odd formations known as "Bigfoot Teepees" at the park; they're strange and puzzling for sure.

In fact, David shows that Bigfoot has been around for a long time in Texas. From the wild woman that was seen around the Navidad River, to early accounts and modern Bigfoot sightings as well, it's all covered here.

Dogmen? Werewolves? Usually, I put them in the same category, but I have come across quite a few werewolf cases in Texas that are *really* strange. One was particularly weird. It took place at the little town of Paradise, Texas. In 1996, a terrified rancher encountered what we might term "an upright wolf." The man was petrified and fled the site. Very intriguing is the fact that the next morning, the farmer found an old carved stone-head on his land. The stone has a creepy looking face and fangs were even carved into the stone.

David covers plenty of other werewolf and dogman cases from the state as well and it makes for a very entertaining chapter.

Now, let's move on to the Texas Chupacabra. Chupacabras originally showed up in Puerto Rico, but those weird, red-eyed creatures have nothing to do with the Texas monsters.

In 2004, around seventeen miles outside of the city of San Antonio, a Chupacabra reared its ugly head. Unlike the sprawling city which is famous for being the home of the legendary Alamo, Elmendorf—the locale—is small in the extreme. For such a tiny locale, unbridled, near-worldwide infamy was waiting just around the corner. There was something very unusual about the Chupacabra of Elmendorf. The famous moniker aside, the Texas Chupacabra looks like a hairless, large dog with a powerful set of jaws and absolutely no fear of people. And so that you know, these things still roam around Texas to this day.

Now what about water monsters? Texas has some. While I have to say that I've never come across a report from Texas about a Nessie-like creature, there are other things swimming around. Giant catfish, massive eels, and the alligator gar could all easily be mistaken for monsters. Then there's "Old One Eye" of Lake Granbury and stories about sea serpents off the coast of Galveston.

Pterosaurs over Texas? That should be the name of a cool band, but we're talking about real, living pterosaurs and the matter of flying enigmas over the Lone Star State. And there are a lot. One of the most famous affairs occurred in 1953 and involved an entity known as the "Houston Batman." It was a creature eerily similar to the famous Mothman of Point Pleasant, West Virginia.

There was also the "Big Bird" flap that involved multiple witnesses who encountered a massive, winged creature. Some people were even attacked by these giant birds.

Like me, David is very much someone who gets on the road, talks to people, and goes to the locations of monster sightings and it shows in his work.

Hideous monsters in the air and water, and massive creatures prowling around make for great reading. If, like me, you have a deep interest in the field of cryptozoology, or "monster-hunting" as it's also known, then you'll enjoy this look into the strange creatures wandering around the Lone Star State.

Now, go look for monsters in Texas!

Nick Redfern

Texas

TEXAS

1845

LONE STAR STATE

Introduction

Texas, known as the Lone Star State, is a unique place. Rich in legend and history, the state sits in the middle of the country along its southern portion, putting it firmly between the south and the southwest of the United States. The state shares influences from both regions as well as having a rich Mexican-American heritage.

Texas is the second largest state in the Union behind Alaska. It ranks second in population behind California and is 26th in population density. Austin is the state capital, and the largest city is Houston, while Dallas-Fort Worth is the largest metroplex in the state. Other large cities include San Antonio and El Paso.

Texas borders several other states: Louisiana to the east, Arkansas to the northeast, Oklahoma to the north and New Mexico to the west. The south and southwestern parts of Texas border several Mexican states: Chihuahua, Coahuila, Nuevo Leon, and Tamaulipas. In the southeast, the state has a coastline along the Gulf of Mexico.

A large number of Native American tribes were present in the land that became Texas from early cultures to more well-known tribes including the Comanche, Apache, Choctaw, Kiowa, Tonkawa, and the Wichita.

The Spanish controlled the region for a long time and the region was controlled by Mexico until the Texas Revolution of 1835-1836. The Republic of Texas was established in the summer of 1836 and remained an independent nation until the 1840s. In 1845, Texas joined the United States and power was officially transferred from the republic to the state of Texas in early 1846.

During the American Civil War, Texas aligned with the

Confederate States of America. While it was far from the major theaters of combat, the state provided a large number of troops to the southern forces.

Texas has a large and powerful economy historically driven by several major industries including cattle ranching, cotton, and timber. The discovery of oil in the state created a massive economic boom for much of the 20th century, creating wealthy oil barons whose families still thrive today. In recent years, the state has seen a rise in tech related businesses.

Other thriving industries in the state include aerospace, biomedical sciences, and tourism.

Hollywood has long painted an image that Texas is a wide-open expanse with nothing but dust, cacti, and cattle, but this is far from the truth.

The state has ten distinct climatic regions. There are Great Plains, large tracts of heavily forested land, a rich coastal region, and much more. Fifteen major rivers flow through the state and there are 3,700 named streams.

Texas isn't typically thought of as full of trees, but actually almost forty percent of the state is forested. These areas include four National Forests: the Sam Houston, the Davy Crockett, the Sabine, and the Angelina.

Texas is also well-known for its wildflowers which bloom in the spring, bringing countless visitors who travel the highways just to take in the colorful beauty.

As for wildlife, Texas has plenty. Mammal species include badgers, pronghorn, beaver, ringtails, armadillos, mountain lions, mountain sheep, prairie dogs, javelina, mule deer and numerous species of bats.

Amphibians include the Southern leopard frog, the Houston toad, the Blanco blind salamander and the barred tiger salamander. There's no shortage of reptiles either. The American alligator can be found in Texas, as can several snakes including the Western cottonmouth, the timber rattlesnake, and the Southern copperhead.

Turtle species include the ornate box turtle, the yellow

mud turtle, and the hawksbill sea turtle. Fish species include the prehistoric-looking alligator gar, blue catfish, pigfish, bass, drum, and countless other species.

Birds are abundant in Texas as well with over 600 species in the state including doves, wild turkeys, several species of duck and goose, burrowing owls, red-bellied woodpeckers, American bald eagles, whooping cranes, and lots of songbirds.

Ranches and private hunting land have, in part, been responsible for importing various exotic species into the state. Some of these include the Axis deer, the blackbuck antelope, fallow deer, and Aoudad sheep.

Then there are the other, unofficial beasts that are said to roam Texas. Bigfoot sightings abound and while the big hairy creature seems to roam freely in the state, there are high concentrations in the heavily forested areas.

But the creature isn't the only strange thing prowling around the Lone Star State. The infamous chupacabra, two versions of it no less, have popped up around Texas and there are even specimens to study.

The Goat Man has made dramatic appearances in the state as well and there are accounts of werewolves—now commonly called dogman. There's also an unseen monster in the Ottine Swamp, and one of my favorites—accounts of living dinosaurs roaming about.

Lest you think the skies are clear, they're not. Tales of giant birds soaring in the Texas skies have long circulated, and there are weird, flying humanoids including the famous Batman in Houston.

So, grab a tall drink, kick back and join me as we explore the Lone Star State's monsters.

PART ONE
Chupacabras & Goat Man

Chupacabra

Chupacabra! Mention the term and people's minds conjure varying images—one, a four-legged hairless canid with a strange, kangaroo-like gait—and two, a bizarre, bipedal thing with bulging eyes, a big head and a line of spikes running down its back.

The evolution of the term chupacabra, which translates to goat sucker, is rather unique in the cryptid world. The first version of the creature is the two-legged, big-headed variety. This alien-like version of the creature first turned up in Puerto Rico in the 1990s and a wave of sightings was reported. The creatures were further described as being grayish to green in color, four feet in height and less than a hundred pounds. They have bulging, black eyes, short forearms that end with a fearsome set of claws, and kangaroo-like back legs. One of the most notable features reported on these creatures is the long series of spikes that protrude from its back along the spine.

This version has, on occasion, been reported in Texas, but for the most part, chupacabra sightings in the Lone Star State are of the canid variety—four legged, hairless with rough sometimes bluish colored skin, a strange loping gait, oddly shaped head, large ears and large fangs, and legs of uneven size.

Purportedly, both versions of the chupacabra survive by sucking the blood from their victims rather than feeding on the flesh, hence the designation "goat sucker."

After the wave of Puerto Rican sightings, reports of the creatures spread to other Spanish speaking countries including Mexico, and then across the border into the United States.

Mexican Americans and other Spanish speakers spread the term chupacabra by applying it to a variety of strange creatures that have plagued various communities around the US, and we can be sure the legend is here to stay.

Chupacabras in the 1990s

On the night of April 20, 1996, Rachel Tolen was driving on a dark road in Zapata County when she saw a weird creature eating something along the side of the road.

Tolen said the creature was about four feet in height and dark brown in color. She saw both skin and hair and said that part of the thing's body looked like it was covered in feathers. She also reported that it had a series of sharp spikes running along its back that started at the back of the skull.

Tolen said the creature turned to look at her and she saw that it had large, glowing red eyes. Still in her vehicle, the woman approached the creature slowly. In a sudden movement, the thing took to the air and flew away.

Jorge Martin reported in *Conspiracion Chupacabras* that other people in the area had seen the creature as well. There were also reported goat and chicken mutilations in the county. The animals were found drained of their blood.

The small town of Donna, in Hidalgo County, was the site of a chupacabra incident in 1996.

Nineteen-year-old Sylvia Ybarra went out one day and found her pet goat, Nena, lying dead in the backyard.

"The goat seemed drained of blood and had deep puncture wounds on its neck. Remembering a television program, Ybarra said, she immediately blamed the chupacabra" (*The Monitor*, McAllen, TX, May 12, 1996).

Weslaco veterinarian Dr. Steve Edelstein didn't think any mysterious creatures were involved in the goat's death. Edelstein said he believed that Ybarra's pet had died from an infection brought on by the bite of a stray dog. He claimed that the lack of blood was due to anemia or the effects of decomposition.

Edelstein's explanation didn't sit well with Ybarra or other members of the community and news of the possible presence of a chupacabra in the area quickly spread. The *Monitor* reported:

"Ybarra and her family still believe the creature is lurking in the surrounding citrus groves, waiting to strike again. News— confirmed or not—travels fast in Donna. Other residents in the community now whisper about the notorious chupacabra. A few people have even hung crosses over their doors to ward it off."

In this case, many people living around the town of Donna thought the chupacabra was of the Puerto Rican variety. "It looks like a weird person with big eyes and little wings," Ybarra told reporters. The *Monitor* further elaborated:

"Some believers say the chupacabra stands on kangaroo legs with porcupine quills along its back. Other witnesses claim the creature has an oblong head, enormous red eyes, and a body covered with thick black hair. Depending on the version, the creature either sports wings or webbed hands" (*The Monitor*, May 12, 1996).

Fears aside, no one in Donna reported actually seeing a chupacabra and the assumption was that the beast was elusive and sly enough to avoid being seen by humans.

The Cuero Chupacabra

Farmers in rural Texas have long dealt with the problem of predators coming around their properties. Livestock and household pets are often easy targets for coyotes, wild dogs, and other carnivores, so ranchers take whatever steps they need to protect their animals.

At her ranch outside the town of Cuero in DeWitt County, Phylis Canion dealt with the problem of predatory creatures for a long time. Something had gotten several of her cats as well as her chickens, but she wasn't sure what the culprit was. She says the predation got worse in the summer of 2007 and the creature was attacking whenever it wanted to. She later stated:

"The scariest thing that happened was the day I found the chicken on my back porch. All the blood was sucked out, and there was not one drop of blood on my porch" (*Victoria Advocate*, July 23, 2007).

Canion also noted that sheep had been found dead on a neighboring property. Like her chicken, the animal's body was devoid of blood.

In July 2007, Canion finally got a look at the elusive predator, and it wasn't what she expected. She caught sight of a strange animal on her property—it was bluish gray in color and hairless, dog-like, but not like anything Canion was familiar with. This in itself was interesting given the woman's background. She and her husband Steve had spent four years living in Africa. During that time, they became very familiar with a wide range of animals and had done a lot of big game hunting. Texas isn't Africa, of course, but Canion was also very educated about wildlife in the Lone Star State.

Not long after she had seen the strange creature, Canion

17

came home to find more chickens dead. Whatever had killed the birds left them where they fell. The rancher found it unusual to say the least. A normal predator would carry its victim off to be devoured, but in this case, the birds had purportedly been drained of blood and their bodies left behind.

Canion set up a video camera hoping to catch footage of the creature. She got plenty of footage of known animals—coyotes, wild dogs, a bobcat, etc…but there was no sign of the elusive, unknown beast.

On July 14th, Canion got a phone call from one of her neighbors who told her that there was a strange animal lying dead on the road near her ranch. The neighbor added that the dead animal was likely the creature that had been attacking Canion's chickens.

Phylis quickly drove over to the location to see what her fellow rancher had found. It was a weird creature to be sure— four legged and completely hairless with bluish gray skin, just like the creature that she had seen running around on her ranch.

While she was examining the thing and trying to discern what it was, Phylis received another phone call letting her know that another one of the beasts had been found dead. This one was right in front of her ranch.

Canion went and looked at the second creature and found it just as weird as the first one. She retrieved a tractor and a bucket and picked the carcass up, taking it back to her ranch for further examination.

The hairless, dog-like animal weighed about forty pounds, had large ears and large, fanged teeth. Canion was surprised by how large the teeth appeared and despite her background, she couldn't figure out what the animal was.

Determined to get to the bottom of the mystery, Canion cut the head off the creature, wrapped it up, and preserved it in a freezer so that she had something preserved to study.

Many people were interested in the identity of the strange creature that Canion had in her possession, and speculation ran rampant. Finally, DNA testing was arranged to determine the

Are Texas Chupacabras simply coyotes?

animal's identity.

So much media attention had been generated about the purported chupacabra that the results of the DNA test were presented during a live television event on Halloween night 2007.

San Antonio reporter Joe Conger hosted the *KENS-5* news special that dramatically showed Conger open the test results to reveal that the creature was—a coyote.

Professor Mike Forstner of Texas State's biology department was also on the special and remarked on the findings:

"The DNA sequence is a virtually identical match to DNA from the coyote. This is probably the answer that a lot of folks thought might be the outcome. I, myself, really thought it was a domestic dog, but the Cuero chupacabra is a Texas coyote."

Phylis Canion disagreed with the results of the test and challenged Forstner to explain why the creature didn't look like a coyote. Forstner said he believed the animal's unusual appearance was due to its having mange.

Canion was so dissatisfied with the results that she later organized another DNA test, this one conducted by experts at the University of California at Davis. The results were slightly different and concluded that the creature was a coyote / Mexican wolf hybrid.

Despite tests that showed the creature was a known animal, there has been a continued fascination with the Cuero chupacabra. Phylis became known as "The Chupacabra Lady," and 2007 became known as "The Year of the Chupacabra." She even had the slogan printed on t-shirts along with an artistic depiction of the creature. She sold thousands of shirts to monster enthusiasts around the world.

LONE STAR STATE MONSTERS by David Weatherly

More Bloodsuckers

In the first part of 2004, rancher Devin McAnally started losing chickens from his property in Elmendorf, Bexar County. McAnally lost around fifty chickens to the unseen creature, and he was no doubt frustrated about the predation.

The killings started with the death of five chickens and quickly escalated to a dozen, then twenty to thirty, and so on. Whatever was attacking the birds was nocturnal and bizarrely, it wasn't devouring the chickens; rather, it was just killing them and leaving the bodies where they fell. The only marks on the birds were puncture wounds in their necks.

Word of the attacks got around, and the area started buzzing with talk of the "Elmendorf Beast." The fact that no one had seen the thing added to the mystery.

Finally, McAnally got a look at the creature that was stalking his animals. Alerted to his dog's barking one day, McAnally looked toward a field and spotted a strange creature moving fast. As Nick Redfern reports in his book *Chupacabra Road Trip*:

"Racing along the fields was an odd, canid-looking animal. The first thought was that it was a greyhound gone wild. At first glance, at least, this was actually not entirely impossible, since a trio of greyhounds had been dumped in the area sometime earlier. The dog theory quickly became less and less likely; the creature ran in a very strange fashion and its coat appeared to be of a slightly blue color. There was something else, too. The presence of both McAnally and his dog seemed to have no effect on the beast. It was apparently fearless about their presence. This, most certainly, was not the typical behavior of the average coyote."

While the animal was soon out of sight, it showed back up

on two more occasions. Each time, McAnally raced inside to retrieve a firearm but by the time he got back out the critter was gone. The rancher decided to prepare himself for the thing's next return and he placed a loaded .22 rifle in a tree fork so that it was close at hand. Soon enough, the creature turned up again. McAnally was carrying some buckets when he spotted the animal. It was calmly eating fruit from a mulberry tree. McAnally quickly went over to his rifle, took aim, and shot the creature, bringing it down with one bullet. The rancher went over to take a close look at the unusual animal. Redfern reports:

"The thing was hardly muscular, in fact, it was probably barely twenty pounds in weight and was hairless, aside from what appeared to be a slight mane that extended along its back. It was the skin that was strangest of all, however; it really was of a bluish color. Vicious-looking teeth, far bigger than those of a coyote, dominated the mouth of the beast. Its tail looked like that of some monstrous, goliath-sized rodent. The limbs did not appear to be of normal proportions. It was, then, a definitive enigma" (Redfern, *Chupacabra Road Trip*).

A bit unsettled by the bizarre looking creature, McAnally put two more bullets in it just to be safe. He had some neighbors take a look at the creature, but no one was able to identify the thing anymore than he could himself.

Not knowing what the thing was, he didn't want to touch it, so he took some photographs and then buried it in red clay in the event it would need to be dug up again later for examination.

There was plenty of speculation as to the creature's identity and the usual suspects were rolled out as possibilities—coyote, Xolo, and wild dog were bandied about. Some thought perhaps the animal was a small Muntjac deer, but of course the most popular opinion was that the thing was a chupacabra. In fact, the creature quickly went from being called the Elmendorf Beast to chupacabra.

Cryptozoologist Ken Gerhard looked into the case and discovered how the name evolved. He explains:

"I found, through the course of my research, that what happened with the name change from Elmendorf Beast to chupacabra is that in an attempt to find out the identity of the creature, pictures were posted up at a local market near Elmendorf. This was a market where many old-timers went. Some of the older Mexican-American people that went into the market saw the photos and began referring to it as a chupacabra. And that's how the name started here in Texas" (Redfern, *Chupacabra Road Trip*).

Gerhard also examined the animal's skull and noted that it was an unusual one. He reported that the skull had a very poor fusion in the jaw area. Strangely, the animal's jaw seemed to be capable of opening in an abnormal fashion, akin to the jaw of a reptile.

Representatives from the San Antonio Zoo eventually got hold of the skull and despite their expertise, none of them could identify the beast, either. It took DNA testing to eventually reveal the nature of the beast—it was a coyote.

In October 2004, the O'Quinn family had a run-in with a weird creature around their home in the small town of Pollok in Angelina County.

Events began when the O'Quinn family dogs chased a creature across the property. The thing dashed for safety and ran into a small crawl space between the ground and the bottom of the O'Quinn's house. The dogs refused to pursue the animal any further, and after some deliberations, it was decided that someone would have to crawl under the house to investigate.

Tyrel O'Quinn went into the dark space and found the creature—one he said was hideous in appearance. Dog-sized and hairless, the creature resembled a rat with large claws and fearsome looking fangs. The O'Quinns used ropes and tried to get the thing out from under their house, but it wouldn't budge. Finally, Tyrel's father, Ben, determined that the only thing to be done was to shoot the creature.

O'Quinn killed the animal, then dragged it out from under the home. Puzzled by its appearance, the family called a relative, Stacy Womack, and told her about the odd beast they had found and shot. Womack worked at a nearby veterinary clinic, and they thought perhaps she could identify the creature.

Curiously, as Womack was driving out to the O'Quinn property, she spotted a creature that matched the dead one she was on her way to examine. The thing ran across the road in front of Womack's vehicle. Womack later speculated that the creature she saw was probably the mate of the deceased animal.

The dead creature was indeed an odd sight. Its skin was bluish, its teeth were huge, and its front legs were shorter than its back legs. Womack and others who looked at the carcass were unable to identify the creature.

According to *Weird Texas* (Shade, Treat & Riggs), one of the stranger aspects of this particular case is that when the animal's head was picked up by the ear, the ear crumbled. The animal's body seemed to be decomposing as if it had been dead for some time, even though it had only been killed hours before.

I find this report especially strange. Did the O'Quinn's miss the creature and end up pulling out a similar one that was already dead under the house? Whatever the case, it's an interesting twist to the Texas chupacabra legend.

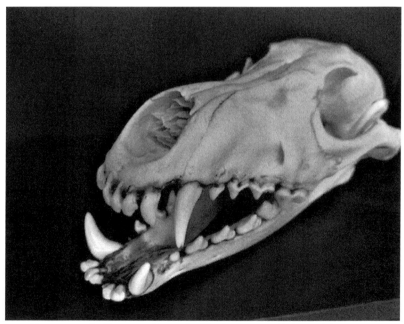

Purported Chupacabra skull given to Nick Redfern

A chupacabra surfaced around the town of Coleman in Coleman County in 2005.

Events began when 89-year-old Reginald Lagow found some of his chickens dead on his property. The man was puzzled by the weirdness of the attack since some of the birds had been partially devoured and others were missing completely. Strangely, there was hardly any blood to be found at the scene.

Several more attacks followed at the Lagow property, then the marauding creature turned its attention to some of Lagow's neighbors' animals.

Lagow saw the thing one day and watched it catch one of the last of his chickens. Unfortunately, the creature got away before the man could do anything. He reported that the beast didn't look like anything he'd seen before and that it had rusty colored hair.

Lagow and other people in the area got some good looks at the creature since it hunted in the daytime, an unusual thing for typical predators in Texas.

Witnesses said the creature was dog-like in appearance and clearly canid. The thing's back legs were longer than its front legs, its ears were large, and its tail very long. Those who observed the creature said that it didn't appear to have mange but did have an odd coat, one that was barely noticeable and looked like soft fuzz that covered its body.

Unlike the typical response of "it's an unknown animal, let's shoot it," Lagow decided to build a trap to try to catch the thing. Despite his best efforts, he was not able to snare the beast and it soon met its end. One of Lagow's neighbors spotted the creature going after his chickens one day and brought it down with a rifle.

According to the August 26, 2005, edition of the *San Angelo Standard-Times*, a dog belonging to one of Lagow's neighbors had cornered the creature in a chicken coop on August 9. The dog's owner shot the chupacabra, bringing an end to the thing's killing spree.

Lagow said the creature weighed around twelve pounds.

He managed to snap a photo of it before the neighbor pitched the carcass away.

Word of the chupacabra had gotten around, of course, and Lagow showed the picture to interested parties. An area veterinarian named Johnny Needham told the man that he'd seen similar creatures before around San Antonio and Conroe.

Needham speculated that the animal had been suffering from "demodectic mange," the result of a mite that burrows into hair follicles and prevents hair growth.

In 2007, a man named Harvey Hayek had some unusual animals show up around his property near Fayetteville, in Fayette County. As it turned out, several members of the Hayek family had seen the creatures and, according to them, the things looked like the chupacabras that had been in the news.

Harvey first saw one of the creatures in the summer of 2007 while he was clearing brush on his land. Hayek was riding on a tractor when the creature first showed up. Hayek told Gerhard that the animal was bold enough to circle the tractor several times as if sizing him up.

Harvey's son Derek was the next person to see the creature. Derek spotted one of the critters in a nearby gulley and took a shot at it with his rifle. Hayek thought he had hit the thing because it went down, but a moment later, it got back up and fled the area.

On yet another occasion, Harvey was shredding brush when he inadvertently disrupted a number of the creatures that were in hiding. The animals ran off toward the nearby Colorado River. Harvey and other family members investigated the area and found what looked like a large bedding spot that the creatures had been using.

Harvey and his wife watched one of the animals hanging around in a gulley one day. The creature was lounging behind a bush, and it was clearly aware that it was being observed as it calmly stared back at the Hayeks.

Ken Gerhard went out to the Hayek property to speak with the family and have a look at the location. He was greeted by the whole Hayek family who all recounted sightings of the creatures on their land. Gerhard recalls:

"Their descriptions were very familiar; the beasts were weird, hairless varmints that seemed to hop around like kangaroos. Several of us drove out to the gulley where most of the sightings had taken place and I was shown a series of large burrows that peppered the red clay and the cliff walls surrounding it. Upon close inspection, I concluded that the burrows most definitely were animal dens of some kind, perhaps an expansive network even, and one that extended deep into the cliff walls" (Gerhard & Redfern, *Monsters of Texas*).

Harvey suggested that Ken poke a long stick into one of the holes to see if anything came out. Gerhard notes: "Being that my profession frequently warrants such potentially hazardous actions, I carefully followed his suggestion, unfortunately, with no result."

In the spring of 2008, my colleague Ken Gerhard was contacted by a San Antonio resident named Greg Davis who said he had video footage of a chupacabra that was lurking in his area. Davis lived on the far west side of the city and invited Gerhard, also a resident of San Antonio, to visit and view the footage. Gerhard took Davis up on his offer and took a look at the film. He reports:

"I witnessed a now very familiar sight: essentially, a weird, hairless canine similar in build to a coyote. The animal was sitting calmly on a paved lot near a wooded area. It got up after a moment or so and trotted off into the brush. Strangely enough, the location was in a heavily populated suburban area surrounding Leon Creek" (Gerhard and Redfern, *Monsters of Texas*).

Davis also told Gerhard that he'd seen the creature a second time a few days later. It was in the same location and, as he observed it, he saw a woman from the neighborhood attempt to give the creature some water and a bowl of dog food. The chupacabra, or whatever it was, fled the area, running across the street and into a subdivision where it was soon out of sight. Davis reported that the animal had not been seen since.

Before he left the Davis home, the man gave Gerhard a gift—two bags of evidence reportedly left behind by the chupacabra—one containing some droppings collected at the scene and another with a severed cat limb found in a pile of fur. Such is the life of a cryptozoologist!

On August 8, 2008, Corporal Brandon Reidell of the DeWitt County Sheriff's Department was out training a new deputy. The pair were riding in Reidell's patrol car driving along fence lines on a country road when an odd, hairless animal emerged from the bushes and ran in front of the vehicle.

Officer Reidell quickly switched on his dash camera and started filming the unusual creature.

The hairless animal trotted along ahead of the vehicle and its odd gait can be seen clearly in the footage. Reidell said that the thing did not run like a coyote and that he'd never seen anything like it before. He also noted that the animal's rear legs appeared to be longer than its front ones. At one point in the footage, the creature turns its head to reveal what appears to be a long, pig-like snout.

Reidell's footage of the chupacabra was picked up by CNN and the broadcast brought national attention to the strange creature.

Reidell later told reporters: "You need to record something like this because it's not every day you find something that looks like this, running around in the middle of the country."

After he examined the footage, DeWitt County sheriff Jode Zavesky was also surprised at the sight of the odd animal. He stated: "You know, it's just kind of one of those things to hear about and talk about, but to actually see something on video that may actually be a live one, that's pretty amazing" (*Banderas News Online*, August 2008).

DeWitt County must have been harboring a pack of chupacabras because a few weeks after deputy Reidel captured the video footage, two more creatures turned up.

The August 31, 2008, edition of the *Victoria Advocate* reported news of the creatures. An area mechanic named Paul

Jones had shot two of the things on his property near Terryville on August 30th. Details revealed that the animals had been in the area for some time. Jones' grandfather had spotted one earlier in August and Brian Wilborn, a friend of the family, had seen one while he was clearing away some brush. A search was launched to hunt the creatures down and on the afternoon of the 30th, Jones shot one of them. A few hours later, the man killed a second creature in the same area.

Several men on the scene examined the creatures and reported that the things resembled both mangy coyotes and the legendary chupacabras that had generated so much media attention in recent years.

Hunting Chupacabras

Late in July 2009, a man living near Blanco was disturbed by the sound of his chickens in distress. From the noise, it was clear they were being harassed or attacked by some kind of predator. The man rushed out to find out what was wrong, but by the time he reached the barn, the attacker was gone.

The man's natural assumption was that he was dealing with a coyote or something similar hunting his chickens and he left out poison that night in the event that the predator returned.

It did return and apparently it took the bait, because the next morning the man found it lying dead in the yard. The problem was the man had no idea what the thing was since it was unlike anything he'd seen before.

By all appearances, the animal was some type of canid. It weighed around eighty pounds and while it looked similar to a dog or coyote, there were stark differences. The animal's front legs were longer than a typical coyote's, for instance. The most startling difference, however, was the coat—there wasn't one. The creature was mostly hairless except for a few tufts around its feet and a line of fur along its backbone. The skin was dark chocolate in color.

The man's cousin, Lynn Butler, came and took a look at the animal, but he wasn't able to identify it either. The men put the creature in a freezer and Butler got in touch with a local friend of his named Jerry Ayer who was a taxidermist. Ayer had twenty years' experience in his trade and the men thought that he would surely be able to identify the thing.

Ayer was intrigued when Butler told him that he may have a chupacabra carcass. The taxidermist took a look at the animal and while he wasn't sure what he was looking at, he did believe it was the same type of beast that had been spotted in Cuero. He offered Butler a trade for the body and in short order, he had it in hand.

It's notable that before Butler let the creature go, he contacted state wildlife officials to make sure he wasn't doing anything illegal in trading the animal to Ayer. Representatives from the state took a look at the creature but they didn't know what it was either and they told Butler he could do whatever he wanted with the remains.

In addition, Texas A & M sent some scientists out to take samples of the body for analysis.

Once Jerry Ayer took possession of the body, he dissected it in an effort to determine exactly what it was. He found that it had canine teeth and the basic skeletal structure of a coyote. He did not initially feel that it was either a coyote, dog, or Xolo. The creature was about ninety-five percent bald and the main portion of fur it still had was between the shoulder blades. To Ayer, the hair looked identical in color to coyote fur.

Ayer taxidermized the animal and put it up at his business in Blanco. Word quickly got out about the purported chupacabra, and Ayer was soon overwhelmed with phone calls from media outlets looking for a story and an interview.

Initially, Ayer thought the publicity would be good for his business, but it seems he vastly underestimated the response that would be generated when news of the cryptid hit the mainstream.

CNN came calling as well as countless other news outlets from New York to Los Angeles and everywhere in between. Some were international such as a radio station from Indonesia. Ayer's little shop was inundated with people anxious to get a look at the mysterious creature.

Ayer's brief media attention was more than enough for his taste. He wasn't really interested in talking about monsters and he turned down interviews, including an offer for an appearance on *Good Morning America*. He had no interest, he said, in going to New York City to talk about chupacabras.

Not only was Ayer over talking about chupacabras, but he was also ready to be rid of the stuffed monster he had on hand. He fielded numerous offers from people wanting to purchase the thing and finally sold it for an undisclosed amount on September 18, 2009. The lucky winner was a part time real estate agent and part time museum curator named John Adolfi.

Adolfi ran a museum in the small town of Phoenix, New York, called the "Lost World Museum." The Blanco beast was put on display in October 2009 under the fitting name "The Chupacabra Exhibit."

Some people thought that Ayer made an odd choice selling the creature to Adolfi. The Lost World Museum is a creationist museum that ties in Christianity, creation and evolution while discussing unusual topics such as aliens, Bigfoot and of course, the chupacabra.

Currently, the creature remains on display in the Phoenix, NY, museum for those who want to get a closer look at the beast.

On the night of January 8, 2010, something attacked twenty chickens at the home of Cesar Garcia in Horizon City, El Paso County. While Garcia didn't see what attacked his chickens, he was shocked to find that there was no blood to be seen anywhere. He states:

"I saw the chickens were dead, but there was no blood around the sheet metal. All of them were just dead in one big pile. But really, I don't know what it was because there was no blood.

"If it had been a dog, there would have been blood everywhere because a dog tears them apart" (*El Paso Times*, January 13, 2010).

The creature, whatever it was, returned another night and killed ten more chickens on the Garcia property. While the attacks were disturbing, they weren't the first signs of unusual activity around the man's home.

Garcia and his brother-in-law Juan Miranda had moved from the Chicago area three years prior, and soon after they were in Horizon City, they began experiencing odd events around their house; mainly, their animals acted in peculiar ways. According to the *Times*:

"Their rabbits went into hiding, their cat spent the weekend on the roof of their house, their roosters didn't crow, and their dogs didn't bark. And at least 30 of their chickens were killed by an unknown interloper" (*El Paso Times*, January 13, 2010).

While the two men were initially reluctant to state what they thought the creature was, they did finally admit that they believed the attacks were carried out by "El Chupacabras."

It's notable that Horizon City already had another monster roaming around its outskirts—namely, a Bigfoot. (See the Bigfoot section of this volume.)

In 2010, a chupacabra showed up on a golf course in Lake Bridgeport in Wise County—or at least people thought one had.

Tony Potter, a maintenance worker at the course located in Runaway Bay, set out to start his workday on January 13 and was shocked to find a strange creature lying dead on the green. The animal had four legs and was almost completely hairless. The skin was tan to brown in color, and it looked like nothing Potter had ever seen before. Potter took the animal to a local veterinarian who also couldn't identify the creature and the mystery grew.

In short order, word got around that a chupacabra had been discovered in the area. Industrious salespeople printed t-shirts, hats and other paraphernalia to capitalize on the monster, but they were soon disappointed.

The January 21, 2010, edition of the *Fort Worth Star-Telegram* reported: "Wise County's 'chupacabra' just a young raccoon."

The paper reported that state biologist Jennifer Barrow had examined the animal and determined its identity. Barrow speculated that the animal had died after falling into the nearby lake during freezing weather. The cold water, she suggested, may have preserved the body and after a time caused the hair to fall out.

The brief monster scare in the city did leave a legacy behind in the form of the "Chupacabra Point Paddling Trail," a paddling area on Lake Bridgeport.

A witness named Sharon told me that she and her mother had seen a chupacabra around their home outside of Houston in 2010. In this case, the creature was reportedly of the Puerto Rican variety—bipedal with a pair of small arms and a number of "spikes" projecting off its back along the spine. The head was big and round, and the eyes large and bulging.

Sharon claimed the thing had "peered into the kitchen window" on two occasions, scaring both her and her mother.

The first sighting was brief, and the creature seemed to be "jumping up and down" to look inside the home. The women ran out of the room and the witness called her brother who lived nearby. He arrived and looked around outside but found nothing.

Whatever the thing was, it soon returned. The witness reports:

"Three nights later, the little thing showed up again. Mom and I were in the kitchen, and we heard a strange slurping sound. We looked over at the window and there it was again, the same big headed, big-eyed creature that we had seen before. I think it was hanging on to the window sill outside because it wasn't jumping that time, it was just staring at us. I screamed and the thing dropped down out of sight and we heard it running away. I went to another window and looked outside where I saw it running. It was on two legs and had a row of pointy things like a porcupine that stuck out its back."

Blanco County—Chupacabra territory

In the winter of 2014, I spoke to a couple living in Blanco County who told me that a pair of chupacabras had hung around their property most of the summer that year.

Oddly, in this case, the creatures didn't harass any of the couple's animals, despite their having a few chickens and a couple of cats. Joan, the wife, did tell me that her cats would often run quickly into the house and wouldn't go outside after dark.

The pair of creatures fit the typical description of other animals seen in the region and dubbed chupacabras—they were canids, mostly hairless, had large ears and a strange loping, kangaroo-like gait.

Joan noted that they had seen a singular creature a couple of times in the summer of 2013, but it didn't hang around. She believed the same one had returned in 2014 with a mate.

The couple showed me the area where they had seen the animals but reported that the creatures hadn't been around for about a month. Recent rain had erased any tracks that may have been left behind.

I checked in with Joan the following year, but she told me that the creatures had not returned that summer.

A family in Ratcliff, Houston County, claimed that they had snared a chupacabra and had it in a cage. They contacted the authorities about the creature. Officials with the Texas Parks & Wildlife Department soon confirmed that the animal was actually a raccoon suffering from mange (*KXAN Austin Online*, June 17, 2023).

Today, many people quickly dismiss the chupacabra as simple folklore or mistaken identity, and DNA testing has certainly shown that at least some of the creatures are coyotes, or coyote hybrids and members of the genus Canis but questions certainly linger, and we shouldn't just dismiss all the reported cases.

If the animals are coyotes, what exactly are they suffering from and what has caused the seeming mutations? It is possible that mange is the culprit in some cases, and it may be passed down from mothers to offspring, but there are other, unusual characteristics that are more difficult to explain—the overly large fangs and irregular skulls, unusually long tails, and the curiously disproportionate limbs.

Perhaps the animals are mutations that have somehow

adapted to their genetic condition and the harsh summer climate of Texas.

And what about the other, even more bizarre version of the chupacabra with bulging eyes, enlarged head and spikes on its spine? How did this weird bipedal version find its way from Puerto Rico to Texas? If it's more mistaken identity, what in the world could people really be seeing?

Ultimately, while we may have some answers, there still seems to be some mystery surrounding the strange Texas chupacabra.

More Bloodsuckers

LONE STAR STATE MONSTERS by David Weatherly

Goat Man

The infamous chupacabra may be fond of attacking goats, but there's a cryptid in Texas that may give the blood sucker a good fight—the Goat Man.

Goat Man accounts have cropped up from numerous locations across the Lone Star State. Just as the name implies, the creatures are reportedly bipedal, man-like goats, or goat-like men, whichever you prefer.

Descriptions of the creatures harken back to the mythical satyr of Greek legend. They're usually said to be human-like in the torso, with the legs and feet of a goat. Their faces are a combination of the two with human features but the horns of a goat.

Interestingly, Goat Man tales are spread out through the years in Texas and not just clustered together. In fact, there's a curious legend from the mid-1800s that, while not a Goat Man, is certainly something odd.

French missionary Emmanuel Domenech reported on the strange goat-like creature reporting, that it was present in central Texas in the 1850s.

Domenech mentions the creature in his book, *Missionary Adventures in Texas and Mexico: A Personal Narrative of Six Years' Sojourn in Those Regions*. He describes it as white with "glossy" fur, about the size of a cat, having claws instead of hooves, and having "rose colored goatlike horns."

Domenech learned about the creature from an officer he spoke with in Fredericksburg around 1850. The man told him that a Comanche woman was keeping one of the animals. The officer also reported that the creatures could be found in the wild in the region.

In Hamilton County there's a Goat Man who's said to live in a drainage pipe on Pecan Creek Trail. The creature reportedly peeks around corners at people who dare to tread down into his den.

South of the city of Belton, in Bell County, a Goat Man purportedly lives in a small cave at Camp Tahuaya.

The camp is a beautiful spot spanning 150 acres with the largest natural spring in Texas on the property. The site is a favorite spot for Boy Scout troops, and if nothing else, the land's resident Goat Man makes for chilling campfire stories.

Goat Man

LONE STAR STATE MONSTERS by David Weatherly

The Lake Worth Monster

One of the best-known cryptid legends in the Lone Star State comes from Lake Worth in Northern Texas.

Lake Worth is a popular recreational area in Tarrant County. The lake is adjacent to the city of Lake Worth which was named after the lake. The area has its own cryptid, aptly named "The Lake Worth Monster."

The creature's legend began in the early morning hours of July 10, 1969, when a group of people rushed into a police station in Fort Worth to report a monster—one they said was half-man, half-goat and covered with fur and scales.

John Reichart, his wife, and two other couples were parked out at Lake Worth around midnight when the creature emerged from the thick brush near the lake. The thing jumped onto the hood of Reichart's car and tried to reach inside the vehicle towards Mrs. Reichart. Fortunately, Mr. Reichart sped away before the Goat Man could get hold of his wife.

Once it was off the car, the creature ran back into the dense woods around the lake leaving behind a foot and a half long scratch on the side of Reichart's vehicle.

Reichart showed police officers the long scratch that the creature had left on his car. Authorities took the report seriously and four patrol cars were sent out to the lake to try to determine what was going on. Reichart accompanied the officers to show them the location of the encounter.

The creature made the news right away, hitting the front page of the *Fort Worth Star-Telegram's* evening edition on July 10, 1969, with the headline:

"Fishy Man-Goat Terrifies Couples Parked at Lake Worth"

The story was written by none other than Jim Mars who would become well known in later years for his books on the JFK assassination conspiracy, UFOs, aliens, and more.

The creature was still in the news the following day, although there was little more to report. Regarding the Reichart party's report, officer James S. McGee told the press: "We did make a serious investigation, because those people were really scared" (*Fort Worth Star-Telegram*, July 11, 1969).

McGee also told reporters that he thought that the Reichart's were the victims of a prank and that it was either someone dressed in an ape costume or that someone had thrown a dummy on the vehicle's hood. McGee did concede to the paper: "That's a dangerous way to pull a prank. Someone is liable to get themselves shot."

As it turned out, the Reicharts and their friends weren't the first people to report seeing an odd creature lurking around the lake. For a couple of months prior to the Reichart encounter, Fort Worth law enforcement had been looking into stories that some kind of weird…something was harassing people around the lake. Some thought that the sightings, at least a portion of them, could be attributed to local teenagers trying to scare people, but the idea of kids in ape costumes didn't really match all the accounts.

Twenty-four hours after the Reichart party had their run-in with the Goat Man, the creature was spotted again.

Jack Harris of Fort Worth was driving near the Lake Worth Nature Center when he spotted the beast running across the road. Harris later described the creature as around seven feet in height and covered with whitish to gray hair or fur. It's important to note that Harris said he heard the creature before seeing it. He recounts:

"We were driving around trying to find (the monster) when we heard it squalling. We heard it before we saw it. [The creature emitted] a pitiful cry like something was hurting him. It sure didn't sound human," Harris added (*Fort Worth Star-Telegram*, June 4, 1989).

Harris wasn't the only one at the lake. As a result of the

news accounts of the creature, eager monster hunters were flooding to the location hoping to catch a glimpse of the thing.

Harris reportedly tried to take a photograph of the creature but the flash on his camera failed to go off and he couldn't capture an image.

Around three dozen locals were also at the lake and they, too, saw the Goat Man. Several people took off in pursuit of the monster as it raced for a nearby bluff. If the posse thought it was going to get to the bottom of the monster mystery, they were in for a surprise.

As it turned out, the Goat Man didn't appreciate being chased by the Texans and he retaliated by throwing a huge tire, complete with its rim, some five hundred feet at the group. The crowd scattered, running for cover and the safety of their vehicles. The previously eager monster hunters fled the area, no doubt now convinced that the lake monster was something more than a teenager in a gorilla costume.

One person who was trying to flee the scene, Ronny Armstrong, was so panicked that he backed his car into a tree.

Police officers found themselves once again at the scene investigating monster reports. At least one deputy who arrived tried to laugh the matter off, but his smirk faded when he, and the others present, heard a strange howl echoing out of the woods around the lake. Like the citizens before them, the officers returned to the safety of their vehicles.

The *Star-Telegram* continued its coverage of the monster that day with the headline: "Police, Residents Observe but Can't Identify Monster."

News accounts, combined with numerous witnesses, led to plenty of stories circulating about the monster. From the summer to the end of the year, somewhere in the neighborhood of a hundred people claimed to have seen Lake Worth's Goat Man.

While many people reported that the creature was covered with white hair or fur, others claimed that the beast they saw was darker in color. Disturbingly, animal mutilations were turning up around the lake. Many of them were the bodies of domestic animals, including some sheep that had purportedly had their necks broken by something unknown.

The Lake Worth Goat Man made a lot of headlines

Would-be monster hunters continued to patrol around the lake, many of them armed with guns. One man claimed that he had shot the Goat Man and hit it. He followed a trail of blood that disappeared into the lake. It appeared that the creature had headed toward Greer Island.

In its July 14 edition, the *Fort Worth Star-Telegram* ran another story related to the monster under the headline: "Ghosts Seen on Greer Island."

The paper reported that a man named Mike Kinson had spotted the monster hanging around the lake, and that he had also seen "misty apparitions," in the area at Greer Island. Greer Island, in fact, is where some people thought the Goat Man lived.

One of the people looking for the creature was a Fort Worth man named Allen Plaster. Plaster went out to the area two to three times a week hoping to spot the thing and his persistence paid off. One evening, Plaster was driving westbound on the lake's shore when a friend he identified only as Kay pointed out the window and shouted that she saw the monster.

The creature that Kay pointed out had stood up from a three-foot-high patch of weeds. Plaster stopped the vehicle, got out, and snapped a photo with his polaroid instant camera.

In hindsight, Plaster said he didn't believe that the photograph was proof of a monster; rather, he thought it was proof of a prankster active at the lake. He noted that the thing stood up as if it were waiting for an opportunity to be seen.

"Looking back, I realize that when we drove by it stood up. Whatever it was, it wanted to be seen" Plaster later said. He added: "That was a prank. That was somebody out there waiting for people to drive by. I don't think an animal would have acted that way" (*Fort Worth Star-Telegram*, June 8, 2006).

The picture became the most famous, well only, photo captured of the monster around the lake. The image shows a large, Bigfoot-like creature with puffy white hair or fur and a small head.

One of the more startling accounts of the monster came

from a man named Charles Buchanan. Buchanan was parked at the lake on the night of November 7, 1969, and was in a sleeping bag lying in the back of his pickup truck.

It's not clear whether the man was simply camping out by the lake, just taking a nap, or out looking for the monster, but whatever the case, he was in for a surprise. Sometime in the middle of the night, Buchanan woke up when a large creature grabbed him and lifted him into the air. Thinking fast, the man snatched up a bag of leftover chicken and shoved it at the monster. Apparently, the poultry was more appealing than Buchanan himself and the creature took it, went into the lake, and swam away toward Greer Island.

During the height of the monster scare at Lake Worth, plenty of theories circulated to explain the sightings. Some people thought the accounts were simply cases of mistaken identity of a known animal. A man named Helmuth Naumer who was employed at the Fort Worth Museum of Science and Nature proclaimed that the Goat Man was nothing more than a pet bobcat that had been released around the lake.

Naumer didn't explain how the bobcat was running around on two legs and throwing tires at those who chased it.

In recent decades, some researchers have come to the conclusion that the creature was probably a Bigfoot and there are certainly some similarities, given the thing's size and the strange howls that were reported. If the creature was/is real and something unknown, a Bigfoot is certainly a strong possibility.

In 2012, an interesting report was posted on the BFRO website from a man who was a teenager in the 1970s and had his own strange encounter at the lake.

The witness says that on December 23, 1976, he and two friends went out to the lake one night to drink some beers and do some fishing. The reporting witness, Robert, was out around Greer Island with his buddies Al and Mike. Robert had parked at a spot where he had fished before and he and Mike were outside the truck putting batteries in their flashlights. Al was in the vehicle with the music turned up loud.

In the next moment, the boys heard a loud vocalization

that Robert describes as a "roar, scream, howl," coming from the woods behind them. After a three second pause, the vocalization sounded again; then there was another pause and then more of the bizarre screams.

Al, still in the truck, had lowered the radio, leaned out and asked, "Robert, what the hell was that?"

The boys wasted no time. They raced from the scene to get away from the unseen creature that was making such loud howls. Robert noted that the sounds echoed and were so loud that "it felt like the woods were shaking." He also reported that the vocalizations sounded "mad as all get out," and that "you could almost hear it [the creature] taking a breath before it howled."

Other cryptid enthusiasts have taken the opposite approach and completely dismissed the entire affair. Well-known Bigfoot researcher John Green thought the whole story was nonsense.

Years after the case, a man claimed that the creature at the lake wasn't a monster but a forty-pound macaque monkey that had gotten loose and was lurking around the lake. If true, one wonders why nothing about the monkey was ever reported during the actual sightings.

During the monster scare itself, many people were of the opinion that the beast was the work of teenage pranksters dressed in a gorilla costume. Of course, just like with the bobcat theory, it's absurd to believe that a teenager in a bulky costume could throw a large tire, with its rim, five hundred feet.

In an effort to dispel the prankster theory once and for all, author Sallie Ann Clarke once offered a reward of several thousand dollars to anyone who could prove they were the lake monster. To do so, they would have to take a polygraph test. Despite the bundle of cash, not a single person came forward to try to take the money.

Clarke was in a good position to make her offer, and she had a vested interest in the topic. Clarke had written a popular book about the creature titled *The Lake Worth Monster*. The book was a blend of fact and fiction, a detail that Clarke later openly discussed and regretted. She told reporters:

"When I wrote it, I hadn't seen the monster. After that, I saw it four times. If I'd seen it before I wrote the book, the book would have been quite a lot different. It wouldn't have been semi-fiction. It would have been like a history" (*Fort Worth Star-Telegram*, June 4, 1989).

In the same article, Clarke stressed that the creature she had seen was a real monster and not someone wearing a costume. "You couldn't make a costume that real," she reports.

Clarke's book is long out of print and difficult to find, but the mystery of the monster has lived on. While commonly known as "The Lake Worth Monster," the beast is also frequently referred to as the Goat Man, or the Greer Island Goat Man, and the Goat Man of Lake Worth.

Whatever you call him, the creature is firmly ingrained in the state's folklore and legend, making it one of the best-known monster tales in Texas.

LONE STAR STATE MONSTERS by David Weatherly

The Goat Man of White Rock Lake

White Rock Lake is northeast of Dallas in Dallas County. The northern portion of the lake is in a state park, while the southern portion was developed over the years with waterfront estates.

The lake is known for its largemouth bass and white crappie but something much more unusual is said to lurk on the shores—a Goat Man.

The Goat Man is purported to be a humanlike creature with the body and legs of a man, a human-like face, and the hooves and horns of a goat. It stands on two legs and is about seven feet in height. The creature's skin is said to have a jaundiced appearance and it has long, gnarled fingers and claw-like fingernails.

The Goat Man has been spotted by picnickers and is typically seen around sunset. It appears from the woods and is known to throw trash and even tires at humans in order to chase them from the area.

Reportedly, the Goat Man at White Rock Lake was most active in the 1970s and 1980s. Given some of the details such as the creature's appearance and purported tire tossing, it's easy to initially assume that people confused stories about the Lake Worth monster and transferred them to White Rock Lake. Before we dismiss it completely, however, it's important to note that there have been at least a few accounts from people who claim to have personally seen something weird at the lake. One of the strangest accounts came from a woman named Sandy Grace who told my colleague Nick Redfern that she had encountered a Goat Man at the lake in the summer of 2001. Grace was out jogging around the lake when a strange creature came out of the woods and moved toward her. The bipedal man-like thing was very large and covered in slight, coarse hair. The creature was a strange sight indeed, as Redfern recounts in *Monsters of Texas*:

"He had the obligatory two horns on his head of a type that no self-respecting Goat Man can ever be seen without. The Goat Man was not intent on sticking around for long, however. After apparently generating a deep and overwhelming sense of panic in Grace, he got down on all fours and disappeared in a flash of light that reminded the witness of a bright camera flash."

The Goat Man of White Rock Lake

The Old Alton Bridge, aka Goatman's Bridge

Goatman's Bridge

The town of Denton is the county seat of Denton County and is part of the Dallas-Fort Worth metroplex. Incorporated in 1866, the city is on the far north end of the metro area and is well known for its music scene, Jazz Festival and the North Texas State Fair and Rodeo. There're plenty of interesting tales to be found in Denton's history and one of the most curious local legends is that of the Goat Man's Bridge."

Formally called the Old Alton Bridge, the iron-truss span bridge once served as a connecting point between the towns of Denton and Copper Canyon. Built in 1884, the bridge remained in constant use until 2001 when vehicle traffic was shifted to an adjacent concrete and steel bridge. The Old Alton Bridge was added to the National Register of Historic Places in the summer of 1988.

While the bridge has a long and important history to the area's communities, it now draws curiosity seekers who are attracted to its bizarre legend, that of the Goat Man.

There are several variations of the legend and many of them fall squarely into ghostly territory rather than cryptid lore, but considering that the tales revolve around some kind of Goat Man figure, it's certainly relevant here.

By some accounts, the legend is derived from the death of a goat herder who was run off the side of the bridge by a group of drunken cowboys. The man and his herd perished in the water below, and since that time, they have haunted the bridge.

Although it involves needless and cruel death, ultimately, this version of the legend is much tamer than the more common tale that's connected to the figure that haunts the bridge.

Most versions of the story involve the lynching of a man

at the site. The victim is often reported as one Oscar Washburn and the hanging dated to 1938. Purportedly, Washburn was an African American goat farmer who was killed by members of the KKK who caught him and hung him from the iron truss. The men carried Washburn out to the bridge, put a noose around his neck, and pushed him over the side. Just after they did, they looked over the bridge and discovered to their shock that the man's body had vanished.

By some accounts, the man's head came off from the force of the drop during the hanging and his body plunged into the water below.

After the man was hung, the killers went to his house and killed the rest of his family. Further impetus, perhaps, for the dead man to return from the grave and seek revenge.

Legend says that it wasn't long after Washburn's death that a weird figure began to haunt the bridge and the woods around it—a figure that was half man and half goat.

By some accounts, the reanimated Washburn, unable to find his own head, tore one off an innocent goat and placed it on his torso, giving him a bizarre hybrid appearance.

Trying to decipher the Washburn story, its variations and various elements, is, at the least, quite challenging, and many of them simply don't add up properly. While the accounts commonly state that Washburn was hung in 1938, claims of the Goat Man figure didn't surface until the late 1960s—a considerable gap in time.

J. Nathan Couch, who wrote the excellent *Goatman: Flesh or Folklore*, did some digging in archives and found a record for Oscar Washburn who was indeed a real person and who was indeed murdered. Washburn lived in the town of Aubrey, about twenty miles from the bridge. However, Washburn was killed in 1917 and his death came at the hands of his brother-in-law rather than a band of hooded riders.

How Washburn's name became attached to the Goat Man legend on the bridge isn't clear. Perhaps it's a case of folklore and history melding together to create urban legend.

One thing is sure, there's a rich body of lore attached to the Old Alton Bridge, including several purported ways to summon and encounter the Goat Man for those who set out to intentionally find him.

Knocking on the bridge's truss three times supposedly causes the Goat Man to appear, standing at the end of the bridge. It's also said that if one parks on the bridge, turns their headlights off, and honks the horn twice, the figure will turn up, or that he can be seen if the seeker drives across the bridge with no lights on. It should come as no surprise to legend trippers that these challenges are especially popular around Halloween when many people believe they are more effective and that the Goat Man is more likely to turn up.

Over the years, there have been various claims of strange, paranormal activity around the bridge. Creepy laughter is reportedly heard as well as splashing in the water below when nothing is there.

It seems that the Goat Man himself is never seen clearly, but typically manifests as a pair of glowing red eyes staring at trespassers on his bridge. Despite purported claims of a goat-headed man being spotted at the site, there don't seem to be any solid reports to follow up on. At least some people who claim to have seen the figure say that it's some kind of supernatural entity that appears and disappears easily.

A Herd of Goat Men

An old legend in the city of La Porte in Harris County mentions a Goat Man that used to lurk on Powell Road. The story reportedly started with a hermit who used to live at the end of the road. The hermit didn't like young lovers parking in the area, and he would often show up and chase them away.

The hermit died under mysterious circumstances and after he perished, a Goat Man figure started turning up to fulfill the hermit's role—chasing away those with amorous intentions who parked on the road.

In his book, *Metroplex Monsters*, Jason McLean writes about a Goat Man legend he learned from a man name Raymond Perez. Perez's older sisters had warned him about traveling a particular road at night. The danger was due to the Goat Man that prowled the area.

The road in question was a popular route for teenagers out for some mischief away from the prying eyes of adults. One encounter purportedly occurred in the mid-1980s and centered around a group of high school seniors from DeSoto High School. The group was headed to a bonfire at Joe Pool Lake. Since they had alcohol in the vehicle, they decided to take a shortcut down Mount Lebanon Road—a poor decision since it's where the Goat Man was said to hang out.

Perez told McLean:

"As they get past Highway 67 and get near Lester Loarch Park, they see this weird creature in the road. It's half man, half goat and almost eight feet tall, and they are going way too fast to stop in time, but this thing jumps on the hood of the truck and is looking into the cab like it's not happy, when the guy driving freaks out and slams into an old oak tree without even hitting the brakes. Surprisingly, the kids, even the two in the truck bed holding the beer and drinks, survived but were all torn up. What freaked out the cops that found them were the hoof prints on the truck's hood and roof."

The *Paranormal About* website ran a report about a Goat Man sighting in Normangee, a town on the Leon/Madison County line.

The witness was roused late at night by the fierce barking of her dogs outside her bedroom window. There was enough light outside for the woman to have a clear view and what she saw shocked her—a Goat Man.

The creature was about seven feet in height. It stood upright on two human legs, had slightly curved shoulders and the horns and hooves of a goat. The rest of the body was like that of a man in shape, but the skin was yellowish-green in color and sparse hair covered the body. The hands, the witness noted, had slightly curled, gray fingernails.

As the woman watched, the Goat Man walked under a pecan tree with the witness's dogs close behind it, nipping at its heels.

Although the witness never saw the Goat Man's face directly, she did catch a glimpse of the side of its face which she said was "nearly the shape of a man's."

The Goat Man left the area quickly, getting away from the pursuing dogs. The woman notes that after the sighting, she would, on occasion, hear what sounded like a goat calling out in the night, even though there were no goats in the area.

Another Goat Man reportedly lurks around Old Foamy Road south of Cleburne in Johnson County. The creature, known as Old Foamy, supposedly haunts the bridge on the route. Like his cohort in Denton, the origin of this Goat Man is at best muddled and difficult to get to the bottom of.

The creature is described as a seven-foot tall, half-man, half-goat who lurks in the woods around the bridge waiting for unsuspecting victims. There's also a supernatural element involved—the creature can reportedly be summoned at will.

The best time for such a ritual is at midnight and those who dare the process are told to park at the edge of the bridge, turn off their headlights, and honk their horn three times.

The Goat Man will supposedly appear on the bridge, walking toward the vehicle while eating a piece of raw meat. If the summoners linger at the site, the Goat Man will throw food and bones at the car, then leap onto the hood and scratch at the vehicle. The only way to escape the creature is by reversing off the bridge to flee the scene.

Richard Dickerson, archivist for the Johnson County Historical Commission Museum, reports that stories of the area's Goat Man began circulating in the 1960s when he was in high school. He reports that the accounts were "mostly the imaginative wanderings of teenage minds trying to spook each other. A yarn heard about the thing coming upon couples making out in their cars at the bridge was the usual trope" (*Cleburne Times-Review*, October 28, 2016).

A Goat Man in Bell County lives in the woods around Fort Hood. The creature gets its kicks by leaping out and chasing vehicles. Anyone brave enough to pursue the creature loses him once he runs onto restricted land around the base.

Yet another Goat Man purportedly hangs out in Bell County. Residents there say that his presence is accompanied by a foul, sulphurous odor that fills the air.

Writing in *Goatman: Flesh or Folklore*, J. Nathan Couch reports that a Goat Man around Matthews in Colorado County stops cars with his bare hands. He's also known to show up at people's doors demanding food.

Couch says there's another Goat Man lurking around Wylie in Collin County that takes a different approach to vehicles—he jumps on the hood and dances a jig!

In the 1990s, a Mount Nebo teenager named Doug Sheldon was hiking out to meet some friends when he reportedly encountered a bipedal, goat-like creature that was howling in the moonlight.

The incident occurred in a rural area near San Angelo. After spotting the creature, Sheldon retreated from the area. He later met up with his friends in town and told them about the thing he had seen. Sheldon's friends didn't believe his story and the group trekked back to the field where the boy had seen the beast. Sure enough, the thing was still there.

Sheldon's account was later reported on the *Monsters and Mysteries of America* television show in 2013.

A Dallas woman told me that she and her mother had seen a Goat Man in the summer of 2014 while driving on a back road close to the Oklahoma border. The witness, Karen, said in her email that she and her mother had left San Antonio that day, headed north to visit relatives. She had worked a double shift prior to the trip so she had fallen asleep while her mother drove. Around eight o'clock, her mother suddenly woke her up. She reports:

"Mom was shoving my arm, making me jerk up quick; then she pointed ahead, telling me to look. I've never seen anything like it. It was a man, but it was also a goat. It looked like statues of the satyrs from mythology. A man's body with arms and hands but a goat's legs and a man-shaped head with goat horns."

Karen says she later learned that her mother had passed the figure already, but had turned around to drive by it again, not believing what she had seen and wanting her daughter to see it as well.

The woman passed the figure slowly, and Karen says that it stared down into the car at her as they drove by. Just as the vehicle turned around again to make another pass, the women saw the creature heading into the woods and it vanished.

The witnesses have tried to rationalize the sighting, speculating that it was a man in a costume, but the explanation doesn't sit well as Karen notes:

"We tried to say that maybe it was some weird guy in a costume, but it sure didn't look like a suit to me, and anyway, why would he be out there in the middle of nowhere dressed up as some kind of goat guy?"

So, what exactly is the Goat Man? Some researchers point to similarities between the Goat Man and Bigfoot in some of the accounts, but for the most part, this doesn't seem to add up. After all, Goat Man witnesses frequently report seeing both horns and goat legs and feet.

Many people dismiss Goat Man legends wholesale, pointing out the propensity of teenagers to conjure things from their imaginations and urban legend, but is that really all there is to the creature?

From the stories we have, it's easy to see that some of the tales have indeed become modern folklore, blending in with the universal bogie man that lurks on lover's lanes, and in some cases, the Goat Man could easily be transposed with the Hook Man, for instance. But unraveling the Goat Man tales is a messy affair. Legend blends with history, with folklore and with modern reports.

Some of the Goat Man tales have a darker bent and dive

LONE STAR STATE MONSTERS by David Weatherly

into the realm of the devilish and satanic. This should come as no surprise. After all, the goat-headed entity Baphomet is now widely used as a symbol of the Satanic temple.

Paranormal investigators, particularly those of a religious bent, who are eager to explore the demonic, quickly leap to the conclusion that any Goat Men running around must have been summoned by satanic practitioners.

One woman who proclaimed herself a medium/psychic/clairvoyant, told me that she knew for a fact that Denton's Goat Man was a manifestation of a goat demon that had been summoned by a coven that did a sacrifice on the bridge.

When I asked her why she believed the creature stayed on the bridge and didn't wander into nearby Dallas, she responded that the Goat Man was "bound" to the bridge and couldn't leave.

Not such a powerful demon after all, I guess.

Still, this idea persists, and the Denton Goat Man has frequently been associated with devilish ritual. Its popularity as a legend tripping spot has led to countless paranormal investigators going to the location to collect evidence, and in some cases, attempting to summon the creature.

In some cases, the group who summed the Goat Man wasn't adept at all. Imagine a group of bumbling devil worshippers inadvertently summoning a Goat Man from some hellish pit. Naturally, since it managed to crawl out of some portal to hell, it has no intention of returning and chooses to haunt a bridge in Texas.

The Denton Goat Man isn't the only one associated with satanic affairs. A Goat Man In Channelview in Harris County was purportedly summoned as a result of satanic sacrifices. He chases people driving on Van Road at night, driven by some dark devilish need.

Another Goat Man who reeks of sulfur lurks around the railroad tracks in the town of Temple in Bell County. This one is said to be on the hunt for children.

All in all, we're left with a series of wild tales and fascinating folklore that seems to branch off in numerous directions. Regardless of what you think of the Goat Man legend, one thing is for sure, the stories aren't going away.

PART TWO
Lone Star Bigfoot

Early Accounts

Given the size of the Lone Star State, it should come as no surprise that Bigfoot sightings are abundant. In fact, there are so many reported sightings that it would take several volumes just to cover them all.

The history of the creature in Texas begins, of course, with Native American nations who had legends of giants in the region. One of the most notable of these comes from the Comanche.

Prior to the coming of Europeans, the Comanche were one of the largest native tribes in the United States. Their homelands ranged from southern Colorado to eastern New Mexico, across southern Kansas, all of Oklahoma and much of northern and southern Texas.

The Comanche spoke of giant creatures commonly referred to by two different names: Piamupits, and Mu pitz. Both names roughly translate to "cannibal monster," "cannibal giant," or "old giant." The monster was a cave dweller said to be twelve feet tall and covered with hair.

Adrienne Mayor mentions the giant legend in *Fossil Legends of the First Americans*, writing:

"He is a fur covered man like Bigfoot. Comanche elders put out food for the Mu pitz because he still roams Oklahoma. Comanches grind Mu pitz bones into a powder and use it to treat sprains and bone problems. They tested the bones first to see if it had special power by putting the bone on their tongues."

The Caddo, a woodlands tribe that inhabited much of what is now northeast Texas, had legends of giants in the region as well. The Caddo referred to the creatures as the "Ha'yacatsi," meaning "lost giants," and said that the things lived deep in the dense, wooded thickets and swamps.

It's interesting to note that much of the region the Caddo once occupied are modern hotspots including the Big Thicket.

One historical Bigfoot account from Texas involves none other than the legendary American frontiersman Davy Crockett.

Crockett has plenty of connections to Texas. Although he was born in Tennessee, his legend is firmly etched into the lore of the Lone Star State, mostly due to his participation in the state's fight for independence and his death during the famous last stand at the Alamo.

In 1836. Crockett, along with other famous figures such as Jim Bowie and William Barrett Travis, and a small number of brave volunteers, held the Alamo against thousands of Mexican soldiers. Although the Alamo fell and the men all perished, their courage served to further spark the drive for Texas's independence and freedom from Mexican rule.

The history of the Alamo is the stuff of legend, but of course, we're here to discuss strange creatures and that brings us to a letter written by Crockett to his brother-in-law Abner Burgin. The letter is undated; however, some of the text implies it was written during Crockett's time in the Alamo. The letter states:

"William and I were pushing through some thicket, clearing the way, when I sat down to mop my brow. I sat for a spell, watching as William made his good and fine progress. I removed my boots and sat with my rations, thinking the afternoon a fine time to lunch. As the birds whistled and chirped and I ate my small and meager rations, I tapped my axe upon the opposite end of the felled tree I rested upon.

"Whether it was the axe's disturbance or possibly the heat of the high sun which caused an apparition to slowly form in front of my eyes, I know not. As a Christian man, I swear to you, Abe, that what spirit came upon me was the shape and shade of a large ape man, the likes we might expect among the more bellicose and hostile Indian tribes of the Territories. The shade formed into the most deformed and ugly countenance. Covered in wild hair, with small and needling eyes, large broken rows of teeth, and the height of three foundlings, I spit upon the ground the bread I was eating. [A foundling is a small child said to have been abandoned by his parents].

"The Monster then addressed a warning to me. Abner, it told me to return from Texas, to flee this Fort and to abandon this lost cause. When I began to question this, the Creature spread upon the wind like the morning steam swirls off a frog pond. I swear to you, Abner, that whatever meat or sausage disagreed with me that afternoon, I foreswore all beef and hog for a day or so afterward."

There are a couple of important points about this account. First of all, Crockett clearly states that he's seeing an "apparition," one that vanishes as suddenly as it appears.

Despite this ghostly aspect, there are plenty of pieces of the story that have excited modern Bigfoot researchers and the creature easily fits the description of a Bigfoot with its wild hair and large stature.

It's also curious to me that the thing appears right after Crockett uses his axe to tap on the fallen tree he's sitting on—a sound that was no doubt akin to wood knocks.

Sadly, as much as I would love to report that this is a significant Bigfoot related document from a historical figure, it seems doubtful that there's any validity to the tale.

The account has been reported in various cryptozoology books and on countless websites; however, there's one big and important issue with the letter: to date, there's no indication that Crockett really wrote it.

Given his place in history, Crockett's trail has been well documented—especially the last period of his life and his time at the Alamo. Historians are constantly on the lookout for anything that fills in missing pieces from the era to further understand the events that unfolded during the last stand. This, of course, includes everything leading up to the famous event.

Given the long and winding path that things on the Internet take, tracking down the original source for a posting is virtually impossible. The nearest we can come to is finding whatever is the earliest dated posting but even this proves difficult with the

Popular lore says that Davy Crockett encountered a Bigfoot

purported Crockett letter.

Indications are that the missive was fabricated, possibly by someone with an interest in Bigfoot, and once it was out there, eager Internet posters did their magic, spreading the tale far and wide.

A legend in the town of Round Rock near Austin in Williamson County says that in the 1800s a young boy was separated from a wagon train of settlers during a stormy night. Rising floodwaters came up from a creek and the settlers had to struggle to survive. In the midst of it, the boy was separated from his parents and by some accounts was presumed dead.

The boy survived, but after the trauma of the event, he went into hiding, retreating from people and becoming a hermit, living in the wooded area around what would later be known as Brushy Creek.

The hairy man was protective of his area, frightening away any travelers that took the route past his home. One day the hairy man's luck ran out and he was trampled down by a speeding stagecoach.

The legend of Round Rock's hairy man didn't end, though. For decades afterward, people reported a hairy man lurking in the area. Teens used to drive up and down the road hoping to catch a glimpse of the famous hairy man and it was a favorite place for young men to bring their girlfriends, hoping that fear of the strange figure would encourage girls to get closer.

In 1994 a festival was started in honor of the hairy man, an outdoor celebration with music, food and a "Hairiest Man Contest."

Unfortunately, Hairy Man Road is nothing like it used to be. Extensive development of the area has changed it significantly and there's little room anymore for a wild man to live.

John Green notes that a wild boy was captured near Austin, Travis County (date unknown).

The boy was discovered wallowing about in a shallow pond and when he was approached, he quickly fled, running about a mile before he was finally caught by some men on horseback. One of the men lassoed the boy who fought back viciously, kicking and striking out until he was brought under control. He was tied up and taken to the home of the man who had first spotted him in the pond.

The wild boy's body was reportedly covered with hair about four inches in length. From his size, it was determined that he was around twelve years old.

According to the report, the boy was not able to speak but possessed the ability to reason. The account says that after his capture, the wild boy followed the man around like a dog.

Reports of a strange animal in Texas appeared in the September 1, 1871, edition of the *Michigan Argus* out of Ann Arbor, MI. The paper reported that residents in Gatesville, in Coryell County, were stirred up about a creature that had appeared in their community. Reports were calling the creature an "orang outang." The *Argus* reports:

"The animal is described as being about seven feet high and covered from head to foot with a thick coating of hair. Its eyes shine like fire, and it boasts of a double row of murderous looking teeth. When last seen it had in one hand a large, crooked stick, and under the other arm a young calf apparently just killed."

Reportedly, a hunting party was gathering to track the creature down and capture or kill it. Typical of such early reports, there were no follow-up stories so we are left to wonder if there was any truth to the tale.

Reportedly, a wild man was caught in west Texas in 1903. He later died and was buried in a local cemetery. Unfortunately, although this account is listed in several sources, there's no additional information or link to a news source detailing where the account originated.

The September 18, 1903, edition of the *Journal* out of Commerce, ran a report dated September 14 about a wild man in Kaufman County. The report, out of the town of Terrell, said that the wild man had been seen near Red Bank. The brief news item says that the figure was large, nude, covered in hair, and had only one eye.

The wild man fled the scene when the group spotted him.

A woman named Ann Bazan recounted a story passed down by her family about a Bigfoot encounter from the 1920s. Bazan's family were Louisiana Cajuns who settled in Southeast Texas. In the 1920s, her father was working as a maintenance man for an oil company, and he had to trek out on horseback to check on the pipelines and take care of any needed repairs. At the time, the pipelines ran through some rugged country, including remote wooded areas and swampland.

According to Bazan, her father was out checking the pipelines one day when he was violently attacked by something "naked and extremely hairy." The creature, whatever it was, had a face and eyes that were "not quite human."

The man said that the beast tried to wrestle his horse away from him but that he was able to fight the thing off enough to make an escape.

The man initially thought that perhaps the attacker was a deranged lunatic living out in the wild, but while the figure's appearance resembled a human, it didn't seem to be a person at all.

The encounter was published in *Weird Texas* (Treat, Shades & Riggs), and the authors mention that the man was haunted by the attack throughout his life, never really knowing what it was he had encountered that day along the pipeline.

The February 23, 1926, edition of Victoria's *Advocate* ran a story posted by the International News Service about a creature seen near Paradise in Wise County. A man named N.E. Stewart said the creature ran on its hind legs and screamed like a wildcat. The beast was reportedly destroying livestock in the area.

Stewart told the Commission that a party had tracked the creature down, but it routed the hunting dogs, then turned to attack the hunters themselves. Reportedly, the men escaped but "their clothes and flesh were torn by the animal."

Some hunters along the Trinity River in Leon County had a startling encounter in 1930.

Two men, Lawyer Henry and another hunter, were hunting

near a fence line when a very large, nine-foot-tall creature came rushing out of the dense brush carrying a calf in its arms. The men estimated that the calf weighed around three hundred pounds, but the creature was running with it without any difficulty. The creature was brown to black in color, and it ran upright on two legs.

The men returned to their employer, a man listed only as Mr. JW, and told him about the incident. At dusk, JW and a group of hunters trekked into the area to see if they could find the creature. The group was accompanied by the local sheriff who had also been filled in on the encounter.

The posse discovered the calf's carcass with the entrails removed. Brush in the area around the carcass was also torn up.

In his report on the incident in *Bigfoot Behavior Vol II*, Ray Crowe notes that three dogs brought to the scene refused to even leave the vehicle, apparently disturbed by the scent or something else they were detecting.

The incident is also listed on the BFRO database, and the report there adds:

"Not long after this occurred, Mr. Lawyer Henry, his family, and many neighbors left the area. A couple of their houses still stand, although in severe disrepair and grown up with brush. The area is still remote and on private land."

Tales of a strange creature in the area go far back in local lore, and it was long known as a troublesome thing prone to stealing hogs and cattle and raiding gardens.

According to the May 28, 1930, edition of the *Texas Light* out of San Antonio, something was lurking in caves near the West Texas Military Academy.

The paper reported that a large creature resembling a gorilla had been spotted near caves in the Olmos Creek Valley in Bexar County. The creature had scared some men working in a rock quarry leading to a hunt for the thing. Several searches had been made, but the creature, whatever it was, proved elusive.

Soon, law enforcement personnel got involved in the hunt for the beast. Parker Spence, assistant city marshal of Alamo

Heights, and J.J. Caperton, a police officer from San Antonio, organized an expedition to search for the unknown creature.

The *Light* reported that the excitement began when a Mexican man, part of a group working at a rock quarry behind the military academy, saw a "shaggy giant, growling ferociously, waddling down the slope toward him."

The man was slightly separated from the rest of the group when he spotted the beast, but at the sight of it, he fled toward the other workers. The paper reports:

"The frightened workman screamed and ran toward the others, who all looked and saw the strange animal stop his lumbering gait, study them for a moment, and then whirl in his tracks and disappear into the brush which lines the quarry."

The men reported that the creature was between four and five feet tall.

Spence and Caperton investigated the scene of the sighting. The paper reported:

"Caperton succeeded in seeing the animal, but the beast disappeared in the thick brush and was lost before the officer could fire. Spence, who was near, heard the sound of the animal as he raced through the thickly grown little valley. A man named Jim Jiminez, who lived in the area, reported that he and his wife had heard 'blood-curdling cries' early one morning, a sound that was presumably made by the strange creature."

The thing's tracks were also reportedly found in the area, though the paper does not provide a description of the prints. It's also noted that searchers found "bits of fur and bones of small animals" in the area where the creature was lurking.

Another search was planned but news of the creature seems to have fizzled away.

A report filed with the Western Bigfoot Society details a sighting from 1938 that occurred in Ellis County. The incident took place in May near the town of Red Oak.

The reporting witness, Randall P. Chapman, noted that the story was originally related to him by his father and that he had heard the tale numerous times while growing up. Chapman said that when his father was eighteen years old, he was out hunting with three other men when they encountered a Bigfoot.

It was between 10 and 11 at night. The group had set up a camp and they were sitting around a fire waiting for their dogs to flush out some game. After a half an hour, the group noticed that not only were the dogs not barking, but they were also refusing to leave the fire, staying close to the hunters' sides, and sticking close to the fire. The dogs were acting very afraid, and the men didn't understand what was going on. Looking around, they soon found out what had the dogs frightened. As Chapman recalled:

"They noticed a huge white-haired figure standing about 30 or so yards from the fire. It was just standing there watching them. Now, my father who lived and hunted in the area all his life never encountered such a creature before."

Seeing the creature, the group of hunters ran from the area as quickly as they could. While it had taken the men a half hour to get back into the thick brush, they escaped the area in about ten minutes.

The trio told other people about the creature, but few believed them. One exception was a man named Tommy who lived in the area. Tommy reported that he frequently heard strange screams echoing out from the bottoms at night.

On another occasion, some of the people who the elder Chapman had talked to about the creature went to the area, drove down a dirt road, and sat there waiting to see if the thing would turn up. It did. The group claimed a large, white-haired beast came out of the woods and headed toward the car. The driver sped away, but the creature pursued the vehicle, keeping pace until the driver reached the main road where he finally lost the beast.

Chapman adds that after the incident, his father never went hunting around Red Oak Creek again.

Gorillas, Critters & Hairy Monsters

As we look at the history of Bigfoot in Texas and follow the trail into modern times, there are plenty of legends to examine.

The city of Jefferson is known as one of the most haunted small towns in America, but it has another, official designation as well—it's the "Bigfoot Capital of Texas." The recognition was granted due to the high number of Bigfoot sightings in the area.

Jefferson might have the official title, but it certainly isn't the only hotspot for the creature. There's the aforementioned Big Thicket and the Sam Houston National Forest, the Sabine River Bottoms and the Angelina National Forest.

Caddo Lake in East Texas is also a hotspot. The swampy lake has a network of woodlands and bayou channels and looks like another world with dark waters and cypress trees draped in Spanish moss.

It's notable that the most well-known Bigfoot themed movie, 1972's *The Legend of Boggy Creek*, was produced and directed by Texarkana filmmaker Charles B. Pierce.

The small town of Fouke, the focal point of the film, is in neighboring Arkansas, but, of course, Bigfoot doesn't pay any attention to state boundaries and there are plenty of reports from areas along the border of Texas and Arkansas.

Modern Bigfoot legends abound as well and there's a long list of regional and local names that have been used for the creatures over the years.

There's the Big Cypress Swamp Monster, the Caddo Critter in Caddo, and the Chambers Creek Monster. Add in Ol' Mossyback, the Athens Banshee, the Night Screamer, and the Brazos Ape-Man, and the list goes on.

Some of the creature legends are completely modern, but many of them go back decades. Haskell County has creature stories that reportedly go back over 100 years. Bigfoot researcher John Green noted of the Haskell creature:

"Residents claim that it spends its summers in the Kiowa Peak area, west of Haskell, and that it prowls in the lowlands during the winter, killing and feeding on livestock" (Green, *Sasquatch: The Apes Among Us*).

Porter Oakes, who was editor of the local *Haskell Free-Press* during a monster flap in the area in the 1960s said that opinions of the creature's identity varied. Some people thought the thing was nothing more than a large bear while others thought it was an escaped gorilla.

Whatever the thing was, numerous people reported seeing it run across roads late at night and it scared several drivers out traversing dark highways with its sudden appearance.

People in Dayton, in Liberty County, have long spoken of a strange creature in their area known as the Monkeyman, or the Monkey Man of 1409. (After FM 1409, a route where several sightings occurred.)

Sightings of the thing date back to at least the 1950s and many families have stories of the beast that have been passed down for years.

The late Rob Riggs, author of *In the Big Thicket: On the Trail of the Wild Man,* spoke to a young man who had encountered the Monkeyman creature one night. The man was at his home near Dayton when he was alerted to a disturbance at his rabbit pen. Rushing outside, he spotted a large, dark creature making off with one of his rabbits. The man pursued the thing into the woods but lost in when it swam across a river, easily making it to the opposite shore despite a strong current.

At one point, the Liberty County Sheriff's Department had so many calls about the creature that they increased patrols in the area hoping to solve the mystery. Despite the increased presence of law enforcement, the beast wasn't caught or even spotted by deputies.

The Raggedy Man lurked between Sour Lake and Beaumont and plagued people parking along a lover's lane. Teenagers attempting to sit in the area for some romantic time found the weird creature staring in through their windshields. The thing was described as man-like but taller and heavier than a man with long hair and a long beard.

In the 2000s, the Sabine Thing was stirring up trouble while it lurked in the densely wooded areas of the county. Like its other hairy relatives, the gray, ape-like creature has so far eluded capture.

Here's a closer look at a few of the notable local Bigfoot legends from the state:

The Navidad River

Wild Woman of the Navidad

In the early 1800s, when much of Texas was still a wild frontier, stories began circulating in Lavaca County that a wild woman was roaming the area.

Settlers living along the banks of the Navidad River in 1837 reported finding barefoot tracks near their homes. The tracks were human-like, and it was clear that two creatures were leaving the prints since one set of prints was much larger than the other. Locals assumed that a male/female pair were wandering about, but they were unsure exactly what the creatures were. After a time, the larger tracks stopped appearing, even though the smaller prints continued to be found. The assumption was that something had happened to the male of the pair.

Although some people speculated that some kind of animal with human-like feet was responsible, most people were of the opinion that a wild woman was roaming about, even though no one had actually seen her. On several occasions, search parties went out and tried to find the woman, but she proved elusive, and no one was able to track her down.

Eventually, further evidence of the wild woman was discovered by accident. A group out driving some cows through the river bottoms stumbled on what appeared to be a den that was being used by the woman. The "den" contained many items that had gone missing from homes in the area. It seems that the wild woman was prone to entering houses and along with stealing food, she frequently took small personal items from the homeowners.

Texan folklorist J. Frank Dobie wrote about the wild woman in his book *Legends of Texas*, and he relates an incident involving a group of men who set out to capture the wild woman once and for all. They took positions along the edge of a prairie while another group drove bloodhounds through the tree line to flush the wild woman out. The creature finally emerged, making a run across the open space headed for the safety of nearby woods on the other side. One man was close to the figure and set off in pursuit hoping to lasso the creature. Dobie writes:

"The man was mounted on a fleet horse, and it needed all its speed to bring this rider to an even race with the object of his pursuit. But the horse was so afraid of the strange creature that he could not be urged within reach of the lasso. Three times he came up, but each time shied to the right or left too far for his rider to throw, while the flying figure each time turned her course to the opposite hand and ran with the speed of a frightened deer.

"Though disappointed in capturing her, one point was gained: the man had a good look at her as they ran together across the prairie for several hundred yards. She had no clothes, but her body was covered with short brown hair. The rider did not see her face, as she was between him and the moon, so that whenever she turned toward him her face was in shadow. Once or twice, he thought he caught a glimpse of wild eyes as she cast a frightened glance over her shoulder. She had something in her hand when he first saw her, but she dropped it either from fright or to facilitate her escape."

Dobie reports that the object the wild creature dropped was discovered at the scene and proved to be "a club about five feet long, polished to a wonder."

A story in the March 17, 1851, edition of Gettysburg, Pennsylvania's *Adams Sentinel and General Advertiser* announced that the wild woman had been captured. The paper relayed information from Houston that a party of deer hunters had come across the wild woman's camp and caught her. According to the report, the wild woman was actually an African woman who had fled to the wild and had wandered the area for around fifteen years. The paper reports:

"Her food during that period has consisted of acorns, nuts, and other wild fruits, with such other food as she could occasionally steal from the neighboring settlements. She cannot speak any English, but converses freely with the Africans on the neighboring plantations."

The paper claimed that the mystery of the wild woman was solved with the discovery, but was it?

Frank Dobie reported that there was another variation of the legend, one that involved a "runaway male slave" who was capture in the area. This also led people to speculate that the wild woman had been captured and, in this case, wasn't a woman at all.

Slavery was a sad reality of the period and there were indeed cases of former slaves who had escaped and were recaptured. This doesn't seem to explain the wild woman of the Navidad, however.

Dobie notes that the descriptions of the creature encountered in Lavaca County differ for several reasons. One, the creature was able to keep pace with, and elude men on horseback, and two, it was reportedly covered with "short brown hair."

On top of that, we have reports from papers of the period with statements such as this:

"Several other persons have repeatedly seen the creature, and they all concur in representing it as a human being, but so covered with shaggy hair as to resemble an ourang otang" (*Daily Sanduskian*, Sandusky, OH, February 12, 1850).

The same edition of Sandusky's paper gives us another version of an attempt to capture the wild woman. In this case, a Mr. Glasscock was involved in the chase. Glasscock had reportedly been on the trail of the wild woman for several days. The man was utilizing dogs in an effort to flush the creature out of the woods. On at least one occasion, he managed to get his lasso over her shoulders, but she slipped the rope and escaped into a dense thicket where she vanished. She was flushed out again at a small prairie. The paper reports:

"Mr. Glasscock states that he was near a small prairie enclosed by the border forests of the river, when the creature emerged from the woods and ran across the prairie in full view. It was about five feet high, resembling a human being, but covered with hair of reddish brown color. In its hand it held a stick about six feet long, which it flourished from side to side, as if to regulate its motions, and aid it when running at full speed. Its head and neck are covered with very long hair which streamed backward in the wind. It ran with the speed of a deer and was soon out of sight. The dogs pursued it and came so close upon it at a small creek, that it was compelled to drop its stick, which was taken by its pursuers. The stick is about six feet long, straight, and smooth as if polished with glass."

While this report bears some similarities to the account reported by Dobie, there seem to be more details along with an indication that the same party made numerous attempts to capture the wild woman.

The paper states that the information it reported came directly from Mr. Glasscock via a telegraph received from Houston.

Beyond this, the case of the wild woman of the Navidad seems to end. News reports ended and sightings trickled away. Some were satisfied with the runaway slave explanation, but others felt there was something else, something far more unusual roaming around the Navidad. Modern researchers are left to wonder if there's something more to the legend.

LONE STAR STATE MONSTERS by David Weatherly

The Sherman Gorilla

In the summer of 1960, residents of the small town of Sherman in Grayson County were worked up about the presence of an ape-like monster that was on the prowl.

The July 20, 1960, edition of the *Sherman Democrat* announced the beast with the headline: "Huge Ape Reported Seen At Blue Creek."

The paper recounted an incident from July 11th involving J.O. Conrad. Around 10:30 that night, just after Conrad had gone to bed, his dog started barking, sounding the alarm that something was on the property.

Conrad told a reporter that he looked out the east window of his home and saw a creature. "He looked to be seven feet tall and about three feet wide across the back," Conrad said.

The thing was standing upright but was somewhat hunched over. Conrad initially thought it might be a man, but as he watched it, he realized it was too large to be a human. The man grabbed a flashlight and a .22 pistol and rushed to the front door. He dashed outside and opened fire as he moved toward the creature. "I know I hit him at least once, but he didn't even flinch," Conrad told the paper.

The flurry of activity had drawn the attention of Conrad's wife and teenaged son. Both went to the window and saw the creature, illuminated in the moonlight. Mrs. Conrad phoned the sheriff's office and reported the incident, telling the officer that her husband was armed and had fired on the creature. Authorities advised against shooting at the animal since wounding it might cause it to turn around and attack.

Mr. Conrad fired his shotgun over the creature's head in order to frighten it away. He says the animal didn't run off but did continue moving, going east down the side of the highway.

Conrad got in his vehicle and pursued the thing, getting a better look at it in the process. The creature continued to walk on two legs as it moved away from the Conrad home. The man told the *Democrat*:

"He looked black as coal. He was real hairy except for his face. I was about 20 feet from him when I shot, and I didn't try to get closer. I was scared."

Conrad followed the creature to the Blue Creek bottoms east of town and watched as it went into the underbrush and vanished. Conrad gave up the chase and returned home.

The story of the monster spread quickly, and the Conrad home was only one stop on the creature's tour through Sherman.

It turned out that the thing had made an appearance earlier that evening about a hundred yards from the Conrad home.

Mrs. Curtis Wilson and her husband were roused by something rustling around outside of their house that night. The Wilson's two dogs were barking in alarm, then suddenly there was a thump against the side of the house. The dogs fell quiet, and Mr. Wilson went outside to investigate. He discovered the dogs huddled in fear in the corner of the porch. Just after, Wilson heard his cows in an excited state indicating that something had them alarmed.

In short order, Wilson heard shots ringing out from the direction of the Conrad home. This caused him to retrieve his own firearm from inside the house. He scoured the area but could find no signs of the intruder.

Grayson County Deputy James Spaugh went to the Conrad home in response to the call from Mrs. Conrad. After talking to the man, deputy Spaugh was convinced that Conrad had encountered something that wasn't human.

The news clipping about the Sherman gorilla surfaced in 2017 when researcher Willie Jacobs discovered it, but the account had been hinted at previously in a March 1969 letter sent to cryptozoologist Ivan Sanderson. A Paris, Texas, university student named Thomas R. Adams wrote to Sanderson about "the monster situation" in northern Texas. Adams said there were numerous reports from the region, including sightings of a "manimal" in Lamar County—a creature that was making "scheduled appearances in June and October." Adams reported that old-timers in the area claimed the creature had been visiting for at least fifty years. The creature was said to be over six feet in height, was prone to peer into windows, and issued a cry like "a man yelling in pain."

Adams didn't call the Sherman beast a gorilla, but he did report that a creature was reported in Grayson County in the Blue Creek area. He writes:

"Most of the reports were early in this decade. They included that of a traveling salesman who watched an apelike creature bound across the highway in his headlight beams, making the crossing in about two strides. Also, the creature was reported in farmyards and around houses late at night, sending dogs into whimpering, shivering fits of fright."

It seems clear from the latter portion of the quote that Adams was aware of the Conrad and Wilson reports and it's unfortunate that there are not more details about the salesman's sighting.

Ironically, a seasoned Bigfoot investigator has lived in Grayson County his whole life—my colleague Jerry Hestand. Hestand was naturally fascinated by the account of the Sherman gorilla. As it turned out, Jerry lived only ten miles from Blue Creek so he started digging in to see what he could find. He soon located James Conrad, the son of J. O. Conrad. James was the thirteen-year-old boy mentioned in the news article. He told Hestand that he'd been the first person to see the creature outside of his window. He alerted his father about the thing and events unfolded from there.

The man told Hestand that the creature was very large in size, well over six feet tall, and covered in black hair. He estimated that the thing was between 400-600 pounds, and he said it stood on two legs the entire time it was in view.

A strange twist came during Hestand's conversation with Conrad. Lyle Blackburn reports in *Texas Bigfoot*:

"James then told Hestand something that seems rather bizarre. 'It was an escaped gorilla from a circus or zoo that was in Sherman,' he said. 'The Grayson County deputies cornered it in Choctaw Creek Bottoms and shot it twice with a .38 caliber pistol. Then the animal was corralled into a large cage and was carried back to the zoo/circus.'"

James Conrad also told Hestand that there had been two news articles published about the Sherman gorilla; one detailing his family's run it with the beast and a second about the animal's capture.

While the information that Jerry discovered is certainly helpful, it adds more mystery to the account. Is the younger Conrad correct, was the creature actually a gorilla?

To date, the purported second news report about a gorilla capture has not turned up. Hestand points out that there are things about the story that don't make sense. The investigator notes:

"I had lived in Grayson County all of my life…I had seen all the circuses that had passed through as a child and I only remember one that had a 'gorilla.' An elaborate poster showing a monstrous, giant ape tearing at his cage was exhibited outside of the venue. Upon entering the exhibit, I saw an undersized chimpanzee that didn't look healthy."

Circuses were frequently blamed for strange animal sightings, whether big cats or "gorillas," and most of the time there's no evidence to back up such claims. Hestand's recollections reinforce the innocence of traveling shows in this case. As for the potential of a zoo escapee, Hestand notes that the town of Sherman doesn't even have a zoo.

Oddly, in August 1960, a brief news item in the *Fort Worth Star Telegram* reported on a gorilla—sort of. The paper's edition for the 10th of the month reports:

"'Gorilla' Really 'Funny' Resident'"

"The 'gorilla' that's been scaring people in the Woodbine area near here was tracked down Wednesday by Sheriff O.E. Whisnand.

Did a gorilla escape a Circus in Texas?

"It turned out to be a 50-year-old man who, as a practical joke, has been donning a gorilla mask, his wife's coat, and a skirt and frightening the daylights out of selected people." (I'm curious as to why he needed a skirt to complete the ensemble, but to each his own I suppose.)

The paper continues:

"The man said he got the idea for the 'joke' from a recent newspaper story describing a big animal recently seen by several Woodbine residents."

The news item is notable since one—it's less than a month after the Sherman gorilla story, and two—Woodbine is only about a half hour from Sherman.

Unfortunately, to date I haven't located any reports about a gorilla or other unusual creature showing up in Woodbine during the period.

LONE STAR STATE MONSTERS by David Weatherly

Caddo Critter

The small town of Caddo in Stephens County is one of those places where everyone knows everyone. It's easy considering the size of the community—the 2000 census recorded forty residents. In some ways, this makes it all the more interesting that the little town has a monster legend involving what locals call the "Caddo Critter."

The creature made headlines in 1964 when the *Abilene Reporter News* announced the latest sighting under the banner "Caddo 'Ape' Seen Again."

The story ran in the paper's July 21st edition reporting that Caddo rancher Charlie Gantt, 72, had spotted the gorilla-like thing near his property. Gantt let loose with ten shots at the creature but still missed hitting the thing. Mrs. Jo Roberts, a news correspondent for the paper, reported that everyone who had seen the creature described it the same—about seven feet in height, four feet wide and covered with hair.

One of Gantt's neighbors told reporters: "If he says he saw it, he saw it! He's never told a lie in his life."

The creature was certainly taking its chances lurking around Caddo as the paper reported:

"Sheriff Chase Booth said Caddo residents are excited about the animal being in the area and are armed with rifles, pistols and shotguns in case the critter makes another appearance."

The critter made headlines again the following day with a longer story that included comments from Gantt who stated: "It looked like a gorilla!"

Gantt specified that the creature had been on his property two nights in a row and that he had emptied a "long-barreled pistol" at the thing.

Responding on comments from doubters, another witness, John Mitchell, added: "Looks like we're gonna' have to kill it and put it under their noses to convince them!"

Mitchell had first seen the creature three weeks prior, and by the time Gantt shot at it, Mitchell had seen it three times. It came out of the mesquite brush near his house and had reportedly fought with the man's dog, swatting the canine to the ground and causing it to run and hide beneath Mitchell's trailer.

A nine-year-old boy named Gene Couch reported seeing the creature as well. The boy was on his way to a fishing hole near his home when he spotted the beast. The boy was so frightened that he ran home as quickly as he could. According to his mother, the boy arrived home "white as a sheet."

Mrs. Couch added that while she hadn't seen the creature herself, she had heard something fighting with neighborhood dogs at night.

John Mitchell's wife heard the boy's story and set out toward the fishing hole to see if the thing was still around. Sure enough, it was, and Mrs. Mitchell got a good look before the beast growled at her and began throwing rocks.

Some Caddo residents thought the whole thing was nonsense and that the figure was either a person or a large male deer, both explanations that the witnesses found absurd.

When news of the critter appeared in the papers, people started to wonder if the thing was the same creature that had been seen in the summer of 1963 in the town of Haskell.

Haskell, a small town sixty miles east of Caddo in Haskell County, had reportedly been plagued by a shaggy monster that was accused of terrorizing ranches and killing livestock.

Haskell's creature was very different in description, however. The Haskell varmint was said to be a quadruped about four feet in height and covered in light brown fur. Some people thought the Haskell creature was likely a mountain lion though this was never confirmed.

The paper also mentioned the "Haskell County Varmint"

aka the "Haskell Rascal." The *Reporter-News* says that people wanted to know how Caddo's critter compared the Haskell's own varmint, so the reporters reached out to Haskell County Sheriff Garth Garrett who responded:

"If the Caddo Critter was an even 4-foot taller, it just could be our varmint walking on his hind legs. Our varmint is known to make 60-mile cycles in its meanderings, and that places the critter well within our rascal's routine prowling territory.

For the most part, the town of Caddo wanted nothing to do with monster news and many people were happy when an explanation, albeit an odd one, was presented.

An area rancher named Cook speculated that the sightings of the creature could be attributed to his missing yak. Cook said the animal had gotten away from his ranch a few months earlier. He told reporters that the animal was tall, dark brown and had small horns.

The yak originally wandered away from a game preserve on the F. Kirk Johnson ranch located near Possum Kingdom Lake and somehow ended up on Cook's ranch.

Of course, yaks are four legged animals with horns—would one really be mistaken for a Bigfoot-like creature?

Whatever the Caddo Critter was, it must have made its way to other pastures because reports quickly died off, or at least people stopped reporting it.

LONE STAR STATE MONSTERS by David Weatherly

Marion County Monster

Monster tales out of Marion County made the headlines in the mid-1960s when a wave of sightings hit the area.

The wave began with a run-in reported by a young man named Johnny Maples. Maples was walking along a rural road near the town of Jefferson on August 20, 1965, when he heard something moving in the bushes. Maples thought it was a friend of his, but when he called out and got no response, he decided it was probably an animal. Maples threw a few rocks toward the sound assuming whatever it was would come out or run away, but the thirteen-year-old got more than he bargained for. In response to his thrown rocks, a large creature burst out from the trees, jumped over a fence, and started running toward the boy.

Terrified, the young Maples boy fled, running as fast as he could to get away from the beast. Looking over his shoulder, his worst fears were confirmed when he saw that the creature was following him. Not only was it pursuing Maples, but it was doing so with ease. The creature was reportedly large enough and had such a long stride that it was able walk at a quick enough pace that it could keep up with the boy.

According to the September 1, 1965, edition of the *Marshall News Messenger*, Maples just kept running, occasionally looking back over his shoulder for glimpses of the beast to confirm that it was still back there. For some reason, the thing apparently tired of its pursuit of Maples. The boy stated: "The last time I turned around the beast had gone off the road and disappeared into the woods. I could hear him moving around but I didn't see him again."

A neighbor came by, picked Johnny up, and drove him home. When Maples told his mother about the encounter, the woman phoned the Marion County Sheriff's Department and reported the incident. A deputy went to the scene but didn't find any signs of the monster.

Young Maples described the creature as seven feet in height and ape-like in appearance with arms that hung to its knees. The thing was covered with long black hair—except on the face, stomach, and palms of the hands.

Given Johnny Maples' age, it should come as no surprise that some people dismissed the story as either a fabrication or the wild imaginings of a boy looking for attention, but the monster wasn't done with Marion County.

The September 8, 1965, edition of the *Longview News Journal* reported on monster related incidents that took place at a cemetery near Jefferson.

Mrs. Mary Manning, her twelve-year-old daughter, Rosemary, and a visitor—Mrs. W. L. Sharp, were at the Old Foundry Cemetery when they heard a strange growl. Although they didn't spot the creature, Mrs. Manning and her husband Herbert returned to the cemetery the following day and found large, unidentified tracks. The Mannings decided to put some fruit out to see if they could attract the creature. They left a bag of green pears on the path near the tracks. Four days later, the pears had disappeared, and a set of fresh tracks were in the ground nearby. Officials quickly assumed that the culprit was a bear but changed their minds after taking a look at the prints. The *News Journal* reported:

"Whatever the animal is, it is extremely large and heavy as the tracks sink into hard ground that even a heavy man failed to dent with his shoes."

The paper noted that Marion County deputy sheriff Bill Freese, who initially thought a bear was to blame, changed his mind after examining the tracks.

Keith Thompson of Marshall also inspected the tracks, and he made plaster casts of some of the prints.

The *Longview News Journal* reported on the monster again in its September 13th edition, posing the question: "One 'Monster'

Or Two?" The paper reports:

"There may be two 'monsters' in the deep woods between this city and Lodi, judging from a report given by a dozen or so hunters and trappers who went into the woods seeking the 'monster' Sunday."

The paper went on to report that hunters had spoken with a man named Bubba Turner who lived near the Old Foundry Cemetery. Turner said that he had noticed his cattle "all in a bunch," clearly frightened of something.

Turner started searching the area, looking for the source of the animals' disturbance. In short order, he found something. Down a path leading to a creek, he spotted not one, but two large black figures. Alarmed by the creatures, Turner retreated and went back inside his home, watching the figures through a window until the things vanished down a trail.

Hunters followed up on the report and inspected the area that Turner had indicated. They found grass and weeds in the area that had been mashed down as well as a bunch of pears that had been picked from a tree in the area and eaten.

Some of the hunters still believed a bear was the culprit while others speculated that a gorilla was on the loose.

One of the most intriguing aspects of what papers had by this time dubbed the "Marion County Monster" was a report linking it to a much earlier sighting—one from the 1920s.

Richard Eason, a sixty-one-year-old T & P Railway conductor, said he believed the creature was a giant ape or gorilla and reported that he'd seen it himself. According to the September 9, 1965, edition of the *Longview News Journal*:

"He believes that he once saw either this 'monster' or one of its ancestors back in 1927 on a cold November night."

Eason recounted that in the 1920s, the T & P Railway was just building the Payne siding between the towns of Jefferson and Lodi. Eason had hopped off the train that November night when it made a stop at the siding. He went to the telephone house which at the time acted as traffic control, passing along messages and orders. The *News Journal* reports what happened next:

"Eason said that when he opened the door to the phone house, in the flickering light from the firebox of the old oil-burning engine, he caught sight of what he thought was either a giant ape or a gorilla and it was standing on its back feet with its arms upraised and teeth bared. Eason jumped back and leaped on the engine of the train."

The train's engineer, W. T. Vawter, and fireman A. C. Capps saw Eason's panicked look and asked what was wrong. He told the men what he had seen but neither of them wanted to get off the train to investigate the creature.

"When I saw that story about the monster in Jefferson, I couldn't help believing that this was the same animal or a direct descendant of the one that scared me out of my wits in 1927," Eason told the paper.

Media coverage of the creature led to numerous "monster hunters" converging on the area and they weren't well received by townspeople. A UPI story from September 20th announced: "Town Fed Up With Monster Hunters."

Jefferson's sheriff, Luke Walker, told reporters that Bigfoot hunters from at least three states had come to town hoping to capture or shoot the creature.

A bizarre addition to the Marion Monster story came in 1970 when the now defunct *Bigfoot Bulletin* published an article about the creature in its October 31 edition (issue 22).

The article, titled "Concerning the Longview, Texas Reports," was submitted by an Army trainee named Nick E. Campbell. Campbell claimed that two of his fellow trainees from the Texas National Guard had told him about Marion's monster and that they had been involved in the hunt for the creature.

The men in question, Private David Lawson, and Private Royal Jacobs, were both from Longview and were there when the events took place. Campbell reported the following to Bigfoot Bulletin:

"In or about the year 1965, there was a rash of reports of

a giant hairy creature roaming the thickets and back country between Jefferson and Longview, Texas, but nearest to Longview. A man and his little daughter reported it as being large, black, and not a bear. Several head of cattle and a couple of people were supposedly killed by it. Private Jacobs was a member of a posse that hunted the creature when he was a teenager. He told me that he saw the body of one of the murdered people and that the victim had been torn apart. At the time he threw his gun back in the car and went home."

Campbell further asserted that Jacobs was a licensed minister, and he would vouch for both men's veracity.

Unfortunately, there's no other information to support the soldier's account. Dwain Dennis, a journalist from Jefferson, followed up on the claim but could find no evidence indicating that there were any such deaths in Marion County that might have been caused by the creature.

While cattle deaths may have slipped under the radar, any strange human deaths would most likely have been reported in the media. As it stands, the Campbell report is an interesting and curious addition to the Marion County Monster tale, but its authenticity is highly doubtful.

Hunters Seek Sniff Of 'Hawley Him'

HAWLEY — Curiousity, stirred by a recent reported sighting of a shaggy, 7-foot, ape-like creature, has sent monster hunters in the Abilene area scurrying for their nets and guns.

Bob Scott, owner of the ranch near here where the creature was reported Wednesday by three youths it supposedly attacked, said he has been contacted by persons throughout the state seeking information concerning the monster which has been dubbed the "Hawley Him."

is nocturnal, since its trail and strong rotten-meat smell will still be fresh.

Nash said the creature should leave a 1½ to 2 foot trail where it has traveled through the brush. But he said the main way he will know if the Hawley Him is in the area is by the rotten smell that accompanies the beast.

"You talk about the odor. It's worse than any rotten meat odor. It will turn your stomach," Nash said.

The Hawley Him in the Abilene news

Hawley Him

On the morning of July 6, 1977, two teenagers were working on the Abilene Boy's Ranch near the small town of Hawley in Jones County. The boys, Tom Roberts (14) and Larry Suggs (15), sat down to take a break at around 10 a.m. Their break didn't last long. They noticed a horrible smell that suddenly filled the area and they heard tree limbs breaking nearby. Seconds later, they were being assaulted by rocks flying through the air. Larry Suggs was hit in the leg by one of the stones, and several of the missiles barely missed the boys' heads.

The pair threw their tools to the ground and ran from the area to escape the hail of rocks. As they were fleeing, they caught a glimpse of their assailant, a giant ape-man creature with huge arms that hung to its knees.

The pair raced for safety and ran to the nearby home of Ed McFarland. They found their friend, fifteen-year-old Renee McFarland, at home and told her about the creature they'd seen. Renee suggested they go back to the site to see if the creature was still there. She grabbed her 30-30 rifle in case the thing was still around. Articles of the period don't indicate clearly whether or not Renee's father, Ed, was at home when the boys arrived, though it seems unlikely since reports indicate that the two boys plus Renee were the only ones that went back to the location of the encounter.

When the trio got back to the area, they discovered the creature was still around, lurking about forty yards away. Renee had intended to shoot the creature herself, but when she saw the thing, she quickly passed the gun over to Suggs and told him to shoot it. Suggs brought the .30-.30 up to his shoulder and fired but he wasn't prepared for the gun's recoil.

The shot missed the ape man, the kick of the rifle knocked

Suggs backwards, and the creature ran off into the bushes. The creature's escape was no mean feat considering how thick the brush was, but Tom Roberts later stated that the thing "just glided through it."

Officials were doubtful of the story until they investigated the scene and found footlong prints in the sandy soil where the boys indicated the creature had been standing.

News of the incident caught the media's attention, and the creature was given the unusual nickname—"The Hawley Him."

Reporter Roger Downing of the *Abilene Reporter News* covered the story and the paper's July 7 edition's front-page headline announced: "Youths Report Attack by the 'Hawley Him.'" Downing wrote that the area where the boys encountered the beast was near a site where twenty-one goats had disappeared from their pen on the property of Bob Scott. Several goat carcasses were later found in the brush near the location.

Officers from the Jones County Sheriff's Office said they thought that coyotes had gotten to the animals, but for Bob Scott and others, the explanation didn't add up, especially since none of the animals were killed in their pen.

But it wasn't just the deaths of the goats that gave credence to the monster tale. The thing had reportedly been around for a time and Renee McFarland said she had seen it before. The *News* reports:

"Wednesday was not the first time Hawley Him has been sighted. Renee said she and two of her girlfriends saw the monster in October during a slumber party. But when she told her parents of the strange creature creeping about the house, they discounted it as a "'trick of the night.'"

Once the media had hold of the story, it didn't take long for news accounts of the Hawley Him to get the attention of monster hunters, many of whom began to converge on the area hoping to bag the beast.

The July 8th edition of the *Reporter News* reported on the

arrival of the monster seekers under the headline "Hunters Seek Sniff of 'Hawley Him.'" The paper noted that two groups had already asked Bob Scott's permission to go after the creature.

Not all the monster hunters were armed. Three students from Abilene College showed up at the ranch and asked Scott if they could "study the creature's habitat."

A man named Ed Nash showed up accompanied by his stepson David Woods. Nash told local reporters that he was anxious to pursue the creature because he'd seen one himself in the back woods of West Virginia in 1964. He said that while the creature was likely to leave a wide trail in the brush when it passed through, he felt that the best way to track the thing was by following the foul odor that it leaves behind—a stomach-turning smell like sulfur and rotting meat.

Nash wanted to catch one of the creatures and turn it over to science for study. Bob Scott gave Nash and his small team permission to search the property for signs of the creature. Nash and Woods, accompanied by a news reporter, searched deep in the woods on the property looking for any evidence of the beast. Nash carried a .30 caliber rifle, and the reporter toted a 35mm camera. Their trek was a difficult one.

The ranch was crisscrossed with game trails, but rain from the previous days had washed some of the soil out, and there were tons of boot prints from people who had launched their own search for the creature without Scott's permission.

Nash and his team did find some unusual footprints. While searching on a long-abandoned dirt road deep in the woods, the men found a fresh track that displayed four toes and the ball of the foot and had a four-foot stride.

Despite Nash's print find and reports from witnesses, Sheriff Woodrow Simmons of the Jones County Sheriff's Department said he doubted that there was anything to the monster reports. Simmons said that no calls about the thing had come into his office about the monster, and the department wasn't following up on the case.

In mid-August west Texas oilman Jack Grimm stepped into the fray and offered a reward of $5,000.00 for the safe capture of the Hawley Him.

Grimm had specific parameters around collecting the reward—the creature had to be an unidentified and undiscovered one and not an escapee from a zoo, circus, or other location.

Grimm wasn't new to monster hunting, having directed money to the search for Bigfoot in the Pacific Northwest and for Scotland's Loch Ness Monster.

In this case, the "Him" remained elusive and no one was able to collect the cash.

Hawley Him

LONE STAR STATE MONSTERS by David Weatherly

Horizon City Monster

El Paso County, in far west Texas, is one of the last places in the state that you would expect to find a Bigfoot legend, but sure enough, the area has one. For years now, locals have talked about a local cryptid dubbed the Horizon City Monster.

Some say the creature hangs out in the mountains while others note that it frequents Lake El Paso, especially at night, looking perhaps, for fresh water to relieve the desert heat.

Accounts of the creature first popped up in the 1970s and have persisted through the years. The September 20, 1975, edition of the *El Paso Times* ran an article on the monster, reporting that it had been spotted by some teenagers near Horizon City's golf course. The teens said the thing was gorilla-like in appearance.

According to the report, fourteen-year-old Billy Fuller and Fifteen-year-old Kathy Ellis were hanging around the golf course one evening when they saw a hairy figure on two legs walking across the green.

Deputy Bill Rutherford was passing by the course that evening and the two teens told him what they'd seen. Rutherford shined his flashlight around the area where the teens had spotted the creature but there was no sign of anything.

In short order, other people reported sightings of the thing. It was typically described as being around eight feet tall, broad in build, covered in hair and having an elongated head and pointy ears. Reportedly, it left behind fourteen-inch footprints.

Fifteen-year-old Bill York said he'd seen the creature as well. He told reporters with the *Times* that the thing's "face was all pushed in and flat like a bulldog's."

York added that the monster had a pronounced nose, eyes that sank deep into its face, and a jaw that jutted out.

Another area teenager was out for a day of hunting not far from the golf course when he spotted the creature. The boy took a shot at the thing with his rifle but missed.

Deputy sheriff Bill Rutherford looked into the reports and examined some tracks that had purportedly been left by the creature. Rutherford believed the tracks were fake, noting that they looked like they had been dug.

Rutherford, who would later become the city's chief of police, believed the entire affair was a hoax. Although he never uncovered any perpetrators, the implication was that the teenagers were making up the monster tales. However, all the witnesses were adamant that they had seen an actual creature.

The news dubbed the creature the "Horizon City Monster," and the media attention brought in monster hunters eager to track the beast down. Interest quickly died down when the creature didn't make any further appearances and the news quickly turned to other things, but it wasn't the end of monster stories in El Paso. In the early 2000s, the creature was in the news again.

The July 31, 2003, edition of the *El Paso Times* featured a story on the Horizon City monster, highlighting reports from a retired secretary named Cecelia Montanez. The paper reports:

"More than two years ago, Cecelia Montanez saw the creature for the first time—more than 7 feet tall, with faded dark brown fur, and standing near Eastlake Boulevard and Darrington Road.

When she saw the gorilla-like creature, it was walking toward the desert. She told reporters that the beast had red eyes and a mouth that resembled that of a bulldog.

Montanez's first sighting of the creature on August 4, 2000, was followed by another encounter in October 2002. The woman says she saw the creature hunched over a dead coyote. When it realized she was observing it, the thing stood up and walked to a nearby mesquite mound. Bizarrely, the thing seemed to vanish into the ground.

Montanez told the paper that she believes the creatures

live in caves in the area, an explanation perhaps for the strange disappearance of the one she saw entering the ground. Local geologists dispute the notion, stating that large desert expanses such as those in El Paso County don't have caverns due to the lack of limestone in the area.

The woman also told the times that she thinks the creatures are vegetarians but survive the desert environment by sucking the blood out of small animals and eating their organs—not quite the definition of a vegetarian.

Lyle Blackburn spoke with a man named Alfredo Hernandez about a 2019 sighting of the area's monster. Hernandez said he was driving on the outskirts of town at 8:00 a.m. when he saw an odd figure walking on the side of the road. He told Blackburn that the thing was "dark, black, lean, and about seven or eight feet tall" (Blackburn, *Texas Bigfoot*).

Hernandez noted that he saw the monster walking about two hundred yards from a water reservoir. No doubt the big creature needed a drink to survive the arid west Texas environment.

A monster may lurk in the mountains outside of El Paso

While the outskirts of El Paso may seem to be an odd place

for a Bigfoot to lurk, it seems that the creature, whatever it is, is sticking around. In the summer of 2021, people reported that the monster was active again and numerous witnesses reported hearing its weird howling.

A disc jockey named Monika with KISS 93.1 FM in El Paso reported her experience with the creature's strange howling. Monika was a cast member for Viva! El Paso's media night at the McKelligon Amphitheatre in early July 2021. While waiting on stage for the show to begin, Monika and other cast members heard weird howling coming from McKelligon Canyon, a canyon located on the southeastern side of El Paso's Franklin Mountains. Writing on the station's website, Monika later reported:

"It must have been around 7ish at the time when out of nowhere, I heard what amounted to a screaming, howling screech in the foreground. Thinking maybe someone was on their phone, I shrugged it off, but then a few minutes later, I heard it again and even asked the cast to stay quiet to see if they could listen too. A minute later, sure enough, the howls came back—one long one, followed by a few short ones."

Monika later listened to online recordings of purported Bigfoot howls and said the sounds matched what she and the other witnesses heard that night at the amphitheater.

Bigfoot Through the Decades

1950s

A report on the GCBRO (Gulf Coast Bigfoot Research Organization) website comes from a witness who related an experience her mother had in Polk County near Segno in the 1950s.

When the woman was a teenager, she and her friends would play hide and seek with their vehicles in the dense thickets of the piney woods. One night under a full moon, the woman and a friend parked down a fire lane and sat for about twenty minutes with the lights off waiting to see if their friends would find them. While they were waiting, they noticed something moving in a field next to the road where they were parked. According to the report:

"As it moved closer to them, they noticed it was walking upright and one of the girls screamed and it took off at a high rate of speed.

"She never played that game again. The creature was ape-like and was dark in color."

The August 14, 1952, edition of the *Kountze News* reported on a man-like creature wandering around the Big Thicket noting that it "had a heavy beard and a hairy body." Whether it was a hermit, wild man, or something more unusual seems unclear and there were no further reports.

1960s

Two girls in Morris County saw a Bigfoot through their bedroom window in the early 1960s.

One of the witnesses reported the incident when she was an adult and gave details to TBRC investigator Charles DeVore. (The incident is also listed on the BFRO website.)

The incident took place at the girls' grandparents' home near Bradfield Chapel, four miles east of Daingerfield. The witness recalls that it was late on a summer night and there was a full moon. The girls heard something walking around outside the window and when they looked out, they spotted a seven-foot-tall creature covered in hair.

The younger sister woke up the girls' grandfather. When the man saw the creature, he retrieved a rifle, kicked out the screen and fired at the thing. The creature issued a very loud bellow or roaring sound, then raced away from the scene, running quickly on two legs.

The witness adds that the thing was large enough to easily step over a barbed wire fence on the property without breaking its stride.

The following day, a search was made of the area, but no footprints or signs of blood were discovered. The woman's grandfather said he didn't know what the creature was, and he told the girls not to talk about the incident.

The property, it should be noted, was an active farm with livestock that included chickens, hogs, cattle and more. The man kept a loaded rifle at the ready to defend against any predators trying to snag one of his animals.

The reporting witness also stated that while she had always enjoyed playing in the woods prior to the sighting, after she had seen the creature, she was afraid to enter the woods or even ride her bike on the gravel road leading to the farm.

The location of the sighting was in the Piney Woods of east Texas, an area with a large number of Bigfoot reports going back decades.

A group of men hunting in Smith County in October 1963 had an encounter that has stayed with the reporting witness his whole life.

The man reported the incident to the BFRO, recalling details of the night of the encounter. The man was a teenager at the time of the sighting. He says that he was out around midnight with four other hunters in an area called the Marlow Bottoms, about five miles south of the town of Tyler. The group's hunting dogs had something treed, and the men followed the barking, reaching the spot where the dogs were standing.

Once at the scene, the men discovered that one of the dogs had its stomach ripped open; although still alive, it was in bad condition.

The hunters illuminated the tree with their lanterns and flashlights and held their guns pointed up and at the ready, unsure of what they were dealing with. The witness recalls:

"We saw a huge animal of some sort, covered in red fur, flaying its arms, and making a dreadful howling noise toward the dogs. One of us, I don't remember who, shot toward the animal and there was a terrifying growl that absolutely scared the wits out of all of us, including the dogs. We immediately left the area at a run."

The man later reports that the creature looked like "a big monkey...around six feet tall."

The shots fired at the creature caused it to scream louder and act more violent and the men and dogs fled the scene. The injured dog survived the incident and the men decided they wouldn't talk about the encounter out of fear of not being believed.

An incident from 1964 is listed on the BFRO website and involves an encounter from Ellis County:

"My father, Kenneth W., and his friend were fishing at a large creek known as Chambers Creek between the towns of Avalon and Ennis, TX, in Ellis County. During this excursion, a large, hulking, hairy creature, approximately eight to ten feet tall, appeared before them and roared, baring its arms. My father and his friend were, of course, frightened nearly hysterically, and proceeded to run, got into my father's truck, and sped ten miles back to Ennis. This so-called "Chambers Creek Monster" was seen by various people following my father's sighting, but since then, it has never been seen again."

Weird Texas (Treat, Shade and Riggs) mentions a story from a woman named Sharon Gossett who recounted a strange experience from Hardin County in the 1960s.

In 1965 Sharon Gossett was part of a group of high school students from Kountze who called themselves the Rat Finks. The group engaged in various teenaged shenanigans, including visits to a cemetery at Old Hardin.

The group had an initiation ritual that involved taking new members to the cemetery to talk to an angel statue. During one such outing, the group spotted a large shadow figure running across the cemetery grounds. The thing ran into a maintenance shed and started tearing around, throwing equipment and other items about.

The noise caused the teens to flee the area but not before they got a closer look at the thing—a large, hairy, ape-like creature, seven feet in height.

The teens were terrified of the beast, and knowing that no one would believe their tale, one member of the group convinced her aunt to go back to the cemetery with them.

The teens and the older woman returned to the location, and they all spotted the creature. The group fled again, but this time, the creature followed them when they left the area. Whatever the thing was, it ran on all fours, keeping pace with the vehicle as they drove away from the cemetery.

Gossett reports that the group dropped the aunt off, retrieved an adult male, and went back to the scene yet again. The creature reappeared but the group had made a poor choice in their guardian—the adult man promptly fainted at the sight of the thing.

Sharon says that the grandmother of one of the teens said she remembered hearing stories of the hairy giant near Old

Hardin when she was a child. The creature was said to lurk in the Cypress Creek bottoms of Hardin County.

A couple that was parked on a dirt road in Angelina County in October 1968 saw a hairy, man-like creature. The man says they were parked near Lufkin in a heavily wooded area when he had the sensation that they were being watched.

"I turned to look out the driver-side window of my car, when I looked straight into the dark face of a very large, man-like, hairy creature which had hunched down to stare at us. It was approximately 6 feet from me."

The creature itself was strange enough, but the sighting was made weirder by the fact that the thing's eyes emitted a faint, pale yellow glow.

The creature had broad shoulders and no distinct neck. Even though it was down on one knee to look into the vehicle, it was still as tall as the man's car.

The man's girlfriend began to scream, and he started the car and sped away, racing to her house where he dropped her off. The following day, the witness and a friend returned to the location of the sighting and searched the area. They found no tracks on the dirt road, but did find some unusual signs in the area. While they were there, the creature showed up again. As the witness recounts:

"The sun was setting through the woods, and I suddenly saw the creature's silhouette between the pine trees. It was following us—silently. I whispered for my friend to look. At first, he couldn't see it, and moved back and forth to scan the thicket. The creature mimicked his movements. After it moved, my friend spotted it. Without speaking, we bolted, ran to my car, and drove off."

The man posted the incident on the BFRO website in 1999, recalling as many details as he could about the encounter.

There were stories of a gorilla-like creature roaming around in Burnet County in the late 1960s. Locals said the bipedal thing stood between 7-8 feet in height and was brown in color. It was frequently seen around Lake Buchanan.

The GCBRO received a report from a man who had a face-to-face encounter with a creature in Upshur County one afternoon in either 1968 or 1969. The witness was 17 or 18 at the time and had gone out hunting with a friend. They were walking through an open field with trees when they encountered the thing. The report notes:

"This creature was asleep under a structure of dead, small tree limbs with mounds of dead leaves piled over the top of it. This mound looked to be about 3 or 4 ft. high. It frightened us so bad seeing an unknown creature like that that we didn't stay long to observe too much but ran straight home. We both had guns but did not even think to use them."

The witness says the creature was between 6-7 feet tall and was on its back sleeping like a human would with its legs stretched out. It was covered with light brown hair and there were no patches of skin visible except on the feet. The witness notes, however, that he did not see the creature's hands, nor did he describe the face or head other than to report that the hair around the head was long.

The structure the thing was in was described as a "hut-like shelter."

"I am just glad we did not wake it up," he notes, stating that he and his friend "turned white as sheets" when they saw the beast and that they quickly fled the area.

"I don't know whether it was dead or not as I didn't stay around long enough to even watch it breathe."

Researcher Mary Green did a follow-up interview with the witness via telephone and learned some additional details, including some notes about the creature's face. According to the online report:

"The mouth was closed, [and he] said it looked ordinary, but was across the face but longer and slimmer than human lips. Nose [was] protruding slightly, looked more like an ape's nose than a human's nose.

"The face was fully covered with hair, as there were NO areas he could see that it did not have some hair of some length or thickness on its face, but still [he] states he did not stare long as he was too terrified."

Green also learned that the structure was at least six feet in length and between 3-4 feet in height.

The report also notes that four months later there was a published account about an Upshur County woman who was driving in the area when a pair of Bigfoot crossed the road in front of her vehicle. She said that one was male and the other female. She also reports that she struck one of them with her car. The impact apparently caused no damage to the creature.

This report was either broadcast or published in a local paper.

A group of people in Hunt County had a terrifying encounter with a Bigfoot one evening in the summer of 1969.

Kenneth Wilson had parked his car by a levee that ran parallel to the South Sulphur River. Wilson was lying down in the back while three of his friends—two women and a man— were taking a walk along the road next to the levee.

Wilson's repose was disrupted when his friends started screaming and came running back to the car in a panic to get out of the area. The group rushed to a nearby gas station where they spoke to Jerry Matlock.

Matlock reported what transpired next:

"It was about midnight, and I had just closed up the gas station where I worked when Kenneth came driving up with some friends and asked to borrow my gun. They said they had seen something down by the levee and wanted to check it out. I thought they were pulling a prank or something and I didn't want to lend them my $100 pistol. So I went along.

"We drove down by the levee and that thing came flying over that levee tearing up everything in the world. He came over that levee squalling and tearing out saplings and ripping up tall grass and heading toward the car" (*Fate* magazine, July 1979).

According to Matlock, the creature was about eight feet in height, taller than any man he'd seen before. It had a "man-like posture" and was covered with brown hair. Its shoulders were wider than a yardstick, according to the witness. The thing, whatever it was, terrified the group. Matlock recalls: "When that thing came over that levee and started squalling, I'd never been so scared in all my life."

Wilson, who was driving, quickly turned the vehicle around and the group fled the area. The man in the passenger seat took Matlock's pistol and tried to fire back at the creature but the gun didn't go off. Matlock speculated that the man was too scared to cock the gun properly since the pistol was in good working order.

The following day, Matlock and Wilson returned to the scene to look for evidence of the creature. They found footprints so large that Matlock's arm, from elbow to fingertip, fit inside the print.

Matlock acknowledged the outrageous nature of the sighting and said: "If somebody was to tell me a story like this, I would figure they were full of bull, but I know what I saw. I was 21 years old when I saw the thing and that's too old to be scared by nothing" (*Fate* magazine, July 1979).

1970s

The *Bigfoot Encounters* website makes a brief mention of a creature known as "the varmint" that lurked around Colorado County in the 1970s. The creature reportedly roamed an area between the towns of Columbus and Weimar. Details are scant but the thing was said to be human-like and covered with hair. It was seen by deer hunters in the area as well as local farmers, but they were reluctant to discuss the beast in any detail.

Multiple witnesses in Bandera County saw a nine-foot-tall hairy creature in 1972 in broad daylight. The creature came from the hills, grabbed a cow, and threw it over its shoulder, then turned and ran away back into the hills. One of the ranchers ran inside and retrieved a rifle, then jumped in a jeep and took off in pursuit of the creature. Despite how quickly the man responded, and the fact that he was in a vehicle, the creature moved quicker and was nowhere to be seen. The witness was stunned by how fast the thing had vanished from the area.

The original source of this account is not clear, though it was posted by researcher Albert Rosales in his Humanoids group on Facebook.

Two men out making propane deliveries in Lamar County in 1972 had a frightening encounter with a creature they thought was going to attack them.

Kenneth Thurman was working for a local gas company and was out on a Saturday night in late fall making deliveries about twenty-five miles northeast of the town of Paris. Thurman had picked up a co-worker to help with the run. The two men stopped on a dirt road close to their first delivery stop to relieve themselves. After being out of the truck's cab for a moment, they noticed a foul odor in the air. Thurman's coworker shouted and pointed out a long shadow moving toward the back of the truck. Thurman turned and saw a creature heading their way at a quick pace. He recounted the moment:

"That thing wasn't four feet from me when I dove into that truck. Listen, I'm a hunter and I'm not scared of the woods or anything in it, but that thing reached out for me, and I was afraid for my life. I don't know what I'd have done if it caught me" (*Fate* magazine, July 1979).

The men jumped in the truck and raced away from the area. As they were leaving, Thurman got a good look at the thing in his rearview mirror. The men rushed down the road and stopped at the house to make their delivery. When they arrived, they found the homeowner sitting on his porch, gun in hand. His hunting dogs were hiding under the house and the man reported that the animals were usually out chasing game. Although the man didn't report seeing a creature, he knew that something was wrong since his hunting dogs were in hiding.

There was still more to Thurman's story. After making the delivery, he and his coworker went back out the way they had come—the only route back to the highway.

Thurman says he drove fifty mph hoping to get out of the area without encountering the creature again. But he did see it again. Just after he swerved onto the highway, he and his passenger saw the thing running through a field near the road, moving in the same direction that the men were traveling.

"I knew that road curved up ahead and I was scared we were going to cross that thing's path when we went around that curve. I said, 'Listen, hell or high water, I'm not going to stop this truck. If that thing runs out in front of us, I'm going to hit it'" (*Fate* magazine, July 1979).

The men were fortunate though. Before they reached the crossing point, the creature took a turn and vanished into the woods. In reflection, Thurman postulated that the thing may have been trying to get away from the truck. Thurman also reported that he was startled by how fast the thing moved and stated that even though he was driving around sixty miles per hour, the creature was still outrunning the truck.

The creature was tall as well. The account states that it stood as tall as the tanks on the propane truck, a height later verified at a little over eight feet.

The men reported the sighting to their company, but they were laughed at so they decided it best to simply not talk about the matter. Someone at the gas company apparently took the account at face value though because a tip was eventually sent to the Dallas Bigfoot Research Society about the encounter.

Investigators spoke with Thurman but since it was long after the encounter, they were not able to investigate the location for physical evidence.

Renowned cryptozoologist and investigator of the strange Ivan Sanderson received a letter from the editor of Commerce, Texas's *Journal*, dated October 5, 1973. The man wrote to inform Sanderson about monstrous activity taking place around the town of Texarkana, in Bowie County. The man writes:

"You will no doubt recall that last summer (1972) near Texarkana, Texas, a reported incident details the sighting of what has been referred to as the Fouke Monster in this area. Subsequently, the Texarkana Jaycees offered a reward of $10,000 for the live capture of this monster. However, the creature has not been in this area since."

Perhaps the creature was worried about the hefty bounty on it, or maybe it just went back over the border to Fouke, Arkansas, since that appeared to be its preferred haunt. 1972, it should be remembered, is the year that Charles B. Pierce released his film, *The Legend of Boggy Creek*, a docudrama-horror movie chronicling encounters with a Bigfoot-like monster that occurred around Fouke. It also bears mentioning that the film was very influential on many people who have delved into the field of cryptozoology.

The editor had more to relate to Sanderson, however, reporting that there had been sightings four weeks prior to his letter (i.e., early September 1973). The man writes:

"Approximately four weeks ago from this date a similar creature was sighted about 7 to 10 miles from here in the South Sulphur River Bottoms near Peerless, Texas. Two such sightings were reported, and one of the persons involved supposedly had photographs of this creature's tracks. They seem to correspond with tracks you described in an interview with the Texarkana *Gazette*."

The April 1981 issue of the *Bigfoot Co-Op* contained a report submitted by Rich Grumley about a November 1974 incident from Bexar County. A man named John Martinez and a friend listed as Rick were hunting outside of San Antonio when they spotted a Bigfoot with long, matted hair on its head. The creature was between 6-7 feet in height. The hunters had a dog with them, and the canine snarled at the creature. No further details were offered regarding the encounter.

John Green recounts a report that was sent to researcher Grover Krantz about a fall 1975 sighting north of San Antonio.

The witness was at a private lake thirty-five miles from the city. He was sitting on a pier on the edge of the water when he heard splashing across the lake. His first thought was that something had fallen in the water, and he looked across to the other side, about one eighth of a mile distance. On that side of the lake was a cliff about 150 feet tall. Looking at the cliff top, the witness spotted a figure, large in stature and gray/brown in color. The man retrieved his .22 rifle and looked through the eight-power scope to get a better look at the figure. He told Krantz:

"It looked to be about eight to nine feet tall, covered with longish hair, more grey to white in color than I had originally thought. I watched it for a good five minutes and got at least a two-thirds front view of the animal or whatever it was. No distinct features such as eyes, nose, ears, but more of a rounded cat's face with hair spreading outward from the center of the face."

The man called a game warden and reported the creature, but the warden dismissed the account, telling the witness that he had likely seen a large goat or a deer.

"The more I thought about the way it moved around and stooped and moved tree limbs around, I couldn't buy the explanation," the witness said.

The following day, the man went across the lake and climbed up to the spot where he had seen the creature moving about. The ground was rocky so there were no prints to be seen, but there was evidence that something had been there. There were broken trees and brush was trampled in the area. The man also discovered a large, flat boulder that had been overturned, one that the witness estimated weighed 300-400 pounds. "I could see no way it could have been overturned by less than three men," he reported.

The November 28, 1976, edition of the *Journal* out of Longview related three sightings from the previous summer that were reported from Hallsville in Harrison County.

One of the reports involved a pair of creatures—one was a staggering twelve feet in height and sliver-haired. Its companion was much smaller, female, and had red tinged hair. The bigger creature was reportedly shucking corn as a human would.

The report notes that the creatures were hanging out around Caddo Lake when they were spotted.

The September 1, 1976, edition of the *San Antonio Light* reported that a man named Ed Olivarri had spotted a seven-foot-tall creature running from his back yard near Kelly Air Force Base (now Kelly Field) in Bexar County. Olivarri was getting ready for work one morning when his dogs alerted him to something in his backyard. He went out to investigate and peered over the fence. Just as he did, a train whistle sounded from a nearby railroad track. The sound startled a creature that had apparently been hiding in the brush and it lit out, running from the scene. Olivarri told a reporter with the *Light* that the creature "looked like some kind of 'Big Foot' monster." He said the thing was about seven feet tall and covered with short brown hair.

Apparently, the creature, or creatures, had been in the area for at least a few days because Olivarri's neighbor, Mrs. Rose Medina, said she'd had an encounter with one a couple of days earlier, on August 30th.

Medina was also alerted by her dogs barking—at three a.m. When she went to the window to see what had the animals excited, she spotted a creature in the glow of her porchlight. Sitting on her back step was a creature about the size of a child covered in light brown fur. It had an ape-like appearance.

Mrs. Medina tapped on the window, causing the creature to leap up and run away, moving rapidly on two legs. The witness estimated it was about three feet in height.

After hearing that his neighbor had also spotted a strange creature in the area, Olivarri searched the woods around the homes for any signs of the things. He found large foot shaped impressions on the banks of a creek in the area but by the time a game warden came to examine them, they had been trampled by reporters and curiosity seekers.

A man on horseback riding in Upshur County in October 1976 spotted a pair of creatures near the town of Gladewater.

It was around 8 p.m. and the man was riding down a dirt road on his way home. His horse began acting strangely, snorting, prancing, and was clearly concerned about something. The animal was so spooked that part of its mane was standing out like it would from static electricity. The man likewise noticed that the hair on his arms and the back of his neck was standing up.

Scanning the area, trying to determine what had the animal worried, the man saw the source—a pair of large creatures standing in a nearby meadow. The creatures were swaying back and forth as if they were trying to catch a scent and determine what was approaching. The largest of the pair was between 7-8 feet in height, while the second one was slightly shorter, an estimated 6-7 feet tall.

The creatures were about 35 yards from the man's position and were behind a barbed wire fence. Despite this, the witness says he was scared, and he promptly kicked the horse into a gallop to get away from the area as quickly as possible. As he was fleeing the scene, the rider glanced back to see the two bipedal creatures walking off into the woods, apparently unconcerned with the rider or his horse (BFRO).

A man told the GCBRO that he had seen a Bigfoot when he was fifteen years old. He was out hunting in Jasper County in December 1977 when the incident occurred.

The man says he was at a deer camp in a heavily wooded area. He had arrived at the camp late, so he grabbed a gun and headed out to a pipeline where he knew a game drive was being made by the other hunters. At about 7:15 a.m., the hunter positioned himself near a spot where the pipeline intersected a dirt road. He sat on a stump and waited. Around fifteen minutes later, he detected movement behind him near a large pine tree. He reports:

"I turned and stared at the tree and could see something peeking from behind it. It would peek from around the tree, then pull its head back like a child playing peek-a-boo. This went on for several minutes. I was frightened because the head that was peeking at me was very high up the tree."

The witness reports that the creature had very long hair around its head that covered its face. After a few moments the thing stepped out from behind the tree, turned, and walked away from the area. The hunter raised his gun but didn't take a shot at the beast. Once the creature headed into the woods, the hunter quickly left the area.

Bigfoot has been seen on remote Texas backroads

Remarkably, the man had a second encounter with a Bigfoot two weeks later. Walking along an old logging road in the same area, he was startled to see a creature step out about fifty yards ahead on the road. It stared at the man for a moment, then continued moving, walking away through the trees.

The man described the creature he spotted as being ape-like, slender but muscular and standing about ten feet tall. Its body was covered with dark brown hair and the witness says the creature acted very curious and "almost playful."

He also notes that it was "eerily quiet" on the morning of his encounter.

A man driving near the town of Commerce in Hunt County in 1978 had to slam on his brakes in order to avoid hitting a seven-and-a-half-foot tall creature that was crossing the road.

The driver reported that he came within a few feet of hitting the thing. It turned and looked at his vehicle, then continued moving across the road and out of view (Rife, *Bigfoot Across America*).

One of the stranger Texas monster tales from the 1970s comes from the town of Vidor in Orange County.

Beckie and Bobby Bussinger were living in a house on a nice, wooded lot in Vidor, a property owned by Beckie's father. Bobby worked for a tire company in nearby Beaumont where Beckie's parents lived.

It was June 1978. The couple had been married for only two weeks and they were just starting to build their life together when strange things began occurring around the property. Although the house was a comfortable one, the Bussingers knew that there had been issues in the area. As reporter John Rice notes in the June 20, 1978, edition of the *Orange Leader*:

"They knew when they moved into the area that previous tenants left because of strange occurrences during the night. An elusive figure roams the night, clawing at the window screens, howling, yelping like a wounded dog."

Sure enough, this is exactly what the Bussingers began to experience. Something, some creature, took to clawing away at the screens on the windows, banging against the walls of the house, and stomping around outside at night. There were also strange sounds including howls and a weird barking noise.

The Bussingers tried to ignore the creature and go about their business, but things escalated quickly. On June 18 they discovered that two of their dogs had been killed and a third had vanished. The following night, Bobby set out to confront the creature and armed himself with a 12-gauge shotgun. He spotted the thing outside—a shaggy-haired beast over six feet in height and muscular in build. The thing headed toward Bobby and Bobby let loose a blast from the shotgun. After he fired, Bobby didn't stick around, he dashed back inside the home and phoned 911 to report the thing to law enforcement.

Sheriff's deputy Jack Reeves answered the dispatch and went to the Bussinger home that night. He arrived at 11:30 to find the couple in a state of near panic. According to the article in the *Leader*, the Bussingers told Reeves that the hindquarters of two of their dogs had been maimed and the animals died. Another was missing and the creature, whatever it was, was still out there. They were scared.

Reeves investigated the scene and saw the torn window screens. Some of the screens were ripped off completely and some of the frames were broken. The damage, the deputy stated, appeared to have been done by bare hands.

Reeves went outside and investigated the yard and the woods. He approached the trees slowly and, in the darkness, he heard strange sounds—growls and howling—in the distance. Reportedly, the sounds were like those of a hyena, or a wounded dog, or something in between. As Reeves moved toward the woods, the creature seemed to back away, retreating into the forest.

Reeves devised a plan. He went back to his patrol car and drove away, parking down the road under a streetlight where he waited to see if the monster would return to the property. He didn't have long to wait. Less than five minutes after he had parked, Reeves's radio crackled with the news that the creature had returned, scratching at the window screens and banging on the rear wall of the house.

Deputy Reeves raced back to the Bussinger home, flipped on the spotlight on his vehicle, and swept the beam across the yard. The creature was already trying to make its escape, but Reeves did catch sight of the thing. The creature was standing about fifty yards away between two small oak trees that formed a vee. When Reeves hit it with the spotlight, the thing quickly moved off into the woods.

Enough was enough for eighteen-year-old Beckie and her newlywed husband. While deputy Reeves stayed with them, the Bussingers packed up some personal belongings and left their home. The couple went to stay with Beckie's parents in Beaumont. Beckie later told reporter John Rice: "I'm not going near that place until they find it. Whatever it is."

A strange addendum to the tale of the Vidor creature involves my good friend Nick Redfern.

Redfern was visiting the town of Vidor and managed to locate the house where the 1970s incidents had occurred. Spotting two people in the home's driveway, Redfern approached and struck up a conversation. Carefully broaching the topic of the monster story, Nick was surprised to learn that the woman he was speaking with was Beckie Bussinger's older sister. The woman gave Redfern a very different version, or side to the story.

The woman told Redfern that there had not been a monster; rather, it was a very human relative of the Bussinger family who, at the time, had been strung out on PCP. Drug use had driven the person to behave like an animal and take up refuge in the woods around the home. She also reported that if anyone in the home had picked up a shotgun to confront an alleged wild beast, it "probably would have been Beckie and not Bobby!"

The information from the interview was certainly surprising for Redfern, and he noted that he found the woman very credible. He also added that he could find "no reason why the woman would find it necessary to besmirch her family in any way, shape or form."

Indeed, it seems that if the woman merely wanted to dispel the monster tale, she could easily have foisted the blame on some nameless drug addict or bum who was in the area at the time rather than pointing the finger at members of her own family!

Two men working in the Angelina National Forest in August 1979 had a daytime sighting of a large creature.

The men were seismic hole drillers and were two to three miles from the nearest road. They had stopped to take a break in an open area at the end of a thickly wooded area.

The first thing the witness noticed was that the woods became strangely quiet. He told Bigfoot investigator Sybilla Irwin: "It became so quiet you could hear your cigarette burning."

Some movement caught the man's eye, and when he looked toward it he spotted a large creature about 100 yards from his position. The creature was covered in reddish brown hair. It walked between 20-50 feet, then went into a ravine and vanished.

The man told Irwin that he had the impression that the thing had been watching the work, perhaps curious about the machines or what the men were doing.

The man estimated that the creature was around 400 pounds in weight. It had broad shoulders and a large chest. The hair was four or five inches long and the beast was at least six feet in height.

Researcher Ray Crowe received a report that Bigfoot showed up around the southwest Texas town of Marfa in Presidio County in October 1979.

A couple driving near the Davis mountains were traveling around 35 mph when they spotted the creature on the side of the road. The driver slowed down to 20 mph and observed the thing as it was caught in the high beams of the vehicle. It was reportedly 7 ½ feet in height, had a large head and a wide, flat face. The creature turned away from the lights but stood on the side of the road and watched the vehicle as it passed.

Marfa, it should be noted, is not a typical spot for Bigfoot sightings and is more known for its mysterious, ghostly lights aptly named the Marfa Lights. Perhaps the creature was in town checking them out for himself!

A man in a boat fishing on the Toledo Bend Reservoir in Sabine County saw a Bigfoot on the shore. The witness doesn't recall the exact year but says that it occurred in June in the late 1970s.

The witness was in a small boat on the Texas side of the

bend when something drew his attention. He noticed a foul odor in the air. He scanned the area but couldn't determine the source of the terrible smell.

Marfa, home to mysterious lights and occasionally monsters

When the witness, D.R., threw his line in the water, he noticed what he first thought was a person watching him from the trees. The figure was on the far bank, a spot that gently sloped upward and was covered with short grass in front of the tree line.

The figure was very still and appeared to be trying to hide. The creature remained still for a couple of minutes, then stood upright, walked out into the open, and looked directly at the man's boat. It then turned and walked slowly up the embankment where it entered a heavy cluster of trees and vanished.

D.R. told the BFRO that the creature was between 8-9 feet in height and was covered with reddish-brown hair except on its face which was bare.

A pair of travelers driving through Lamar County in November 1979 had a sighting near the town of Direct. The reporting witness was in the passenger seat of the vehicle and the pair were traveling down a one lane gravel road in the Direct Bottoms. The witness told the BFRO:

"We saw, less than 100 feet away from us, a creature cross the road from the left side of the road to the right. It was 7 to 8 feet tall, with long gray hair. It walked right in front of us. Its arms were longer than a man's, swinging them as it walked. It stepped right over a barbed-wire fence."

The witness added that the creature's hair was light gray and lay down smoothly on the body from head to toe. She also notes that the creature did not seem to react to the vehicle's approach and walked in a slow manner.

In the spring of either 1979 or 1980, a couple parked in a remote area of Liberty County had a large creature approach their vehicle.

The reporting witness says he had taken a young lady to a spot east of Highway 59 for some alone time. The man parked on a pipeline and the couple were at the spot for about forty-five minutes when the man heard something rustling in the undergrowth.

"I sat up and turned on the headlights and saw a very large creature standing about six feet from the front of the truck. It stood at least seven feet tall and possibly taller, was covered in dark brown or reddish-brown hair."

The man started the vehicle and backed away from the creature. He turned around to get another look at the thing, but it had vanished.

The witness told Bigfoot investigator Sybilla Irwin that the creature was muscular with massive shoulders and that it probably weighed between 350-400 pounds.

1980s

On September 10, 1980, two men in Travis County saw a bipedal creature near the Pedernales River.

The men were on Old Ferry Road near Paleface Park when something big and hairy trotted across the road. One of the men quickly locked the vehicle's doors.

The sighting was around dusk, and the creature was about 75 yards ahead of the vehicle moving on two legs.

The reporting witness told the BFRO that he and his friend were so scared that they immediately left the area and headed home. A few days later, the men spoke with an officer from the Travis County sheriff's office. The officer told the men it was likely a bear since he'd recently seen one in the area himself.

The witness is insistent that the creature was not a bear. It stood between 6-8 feet in height, was brown in color and "trotted" on two legs. The witness adds:

"We did not hear or smell anything due to the fact we were in the car, but it sure scared the daylights out of us. We often fished the Pedernales River at night and heard lots of unexplained howls and screams that would make the hair stand up on the back of your neck."

Two cousins out at a remote farm in Cherokee County spotted a Bigfoot moving around during a thunderstorm in the spring of 1981.

The two witnesses were fishing on a lake on the property when a storm started coming in. They left the fish they had caught on a stringer in the water and tied it to a tree on the lake's shore, then they retreated into a barn about 100 yards from the lake to wait out the storm.

While waiting in the barn, the reporting witness looked out toward the lake and saw a large creature illuminated by flashes of lightning. The creature was 7-8 feet in height and walked fast, swinging its arms as it moved. The thing was bipedal, dark in color and moved in a "purposeful motion." The creature took long strides of 4-5 feet between steps.

The reporting witness told the BFRO that he's now a veterinarian and has been around animals his whole life. He remains puzzled as to why the creature was moving around during a thunderstorm since most animals take cover during such events.

The men remained in the barn until morning. When they went to retrieve the stinger of fish they had caught, they discovered that the fish had been eaten with only the heads and bones left behind.

The witness told his grandmother about the sighting since it was on her property. She told him that he'd probably seen a Bigfoot, adding that she had seen them herself many times when she was growing up in South Houston County in the Big Thicket.

A couple driving in Newton County in November (1981 or 1982, they aren't sure of the year), saw a large creature cross the road in front of their vehicle a couple of miles from the town of Bon Wier.

The couple were driving on Highway 190 headed to Nacogdoches after a Thanksgiving outing.

The creature was lean and hairy, and the reporting witness says it appeared yellow in his headlights, but he believes it was actually gray to silver in color.

The thing calmly walked to the center of the road, paused, looked in the direction of the oncoming vehicle, then continued to move to the opposite side of the highway, moving from east to west.

The witness added that the creature had long arms, a hairy face, hands and feet, and a head that was more round than conical (BFRO).

I received a report from a man named Drew who also saw a Bigfoot near the Pedernales River in Travis County.

Drew's sighting was in the fall of 1982 and was near Paleface Park in Spicewood, the same area as the 1980 sighting recounted previously.

Drew had just exited his vehicle and walked around to

the back. He was about to open the trunk when he had an odd feeling. He recalls:

The Pedernales

"The hair went up on the back of my neck. I stood there with my hand on the trunk and looked around. You know that feeling that someone is watching you or something bad is about to happen? That's what I felt."

As Drew stood by his vehicle he scanned the area, trying to determine the source of his uneasy feelings. He grew more concerned when he suddenly realized that the area was "dead silent." Normally the area is alive with the sounds of birds, squirrels, insects, and other wildlife, but on this occasion, there was an eerie quiet. A noise then broke the silence; something was moving through the brush ahead of him and on his left. He reports:

"This...thing came out of nowhere. It looked sort of like a big ape but more lean and not bulky like a gorilla. It was on two legs. It looked at me and it looked pissed off. I must have been white as a sheet, and I couldn't move. I was just terrified. It was so big and looked so mean."

Drew says the creature stared him down for what seemed like several minutes, but, he admits, it was probably only a few seconds. The thing walked across the road going toward the river. As soon as it hit the brush on the other side Drew jumped into the driver's seat of his car and sped away. He says that he initially reversed down the road, not wanting to drive past the spot where the creature had emerged.

He stopped going to the river and tried his best to forget the incident. A couple of years later he saw a depiction of Bigfoot and realized that it matched what he saw that day along the Pedernales.

He said the creature was covered with long hair that was reddish-brown in color. It stood on two legs and was roughly seven feet in height. The face was "like an angry ape" and the head was slightly pointed on top. The arms were long and swung as it moved. The thing took long strides when it crossed the road. The witness didn't notice any odor during the encounter.

An incident from the summer of 1983 involves multiple creatures that were active around a home construction site.

The reporting witness told the BFRO that he had purchased a lot in a new subdivision in Montgomery County and that he and his brother were building the house themselves. He notes that the lot was in an empty portion of the subdivision and that there was swamp behind his parcel.

The two men were at the site one night when they noticed a smell that the witness said was like that of a "bad potato." The men heard something very large moving around them and they noticed that there was complete silence in the area save for the noise of the movement. They did not see the creature that was moving around, and it soon left the area.

Things became more intense the following night. The two men had finished working for the day and were hoping to relax a bit. Night fell and the pair were sitting back in lawn chairs. They had their lanterns off and were enjoying the night, but the peace was broken. The witness reports:

"It had been very quiet but about fifty yards to the side of us all hell broke loose. There were at least three very large animals [that] began to scream and cackle and make a primate type babbling."

The man says the sounds were frightening and that in the following days and nights, the creatures remained around the area, observing the men during the daylight, but keeping their distance.

The witness reports seeing a creature he believes was a large male, eight feet in height with broad shoulders and a sloping forehead.

The witness added that the area of the encounters was about three miles from the San Jacinto River and that at the time the area was mostly undeveloped and included heavy clusters of pine trees and swamps.

The GCBRO received a report about an incident from December 1983. Two hunters were out near Alto in Cherokee County between 4:30 and 5:00 p.m. one day when they encountered a strange creature. The reporting witness states:

"As my good friend Brad Dominy and I were out deer hunting one afternoon, we were walking out behind his dad's dairy barn going to the creek to catch the deer as they came down to drink before bedding down for the night. As we crossed a clearing, I saw something very tall and covered with dark brown hair."

The witness pointed the figure out to his friend who didn't see it at first. The pair began shouting to find out if it was a man. They were shocked when, in response, the creature started screaming. The reporting witness was unnerved by the response and fired his shotgun in the air attempting to scare the beast away.

"After I fired, the scream turned into a very demonic sounding growl."

The creature then stormed out of the woods and the witnesses got a good look at it. The thing stood about seven feet tall, was covered in dark brown hair and had broad shoulders.

The two hunters quickly fled the scene. The witness reports that having grown up hunting in the area, he was confident that the animal was not a bear.

Several days later, in the same area, two calves were found disemboweled.

The witness notes: "To this day, Brad will not even admit that we saw anything as he thinks people will call [us] crazy."

A hunter in Bowie County spotted a Bigfoot one afternoon in November 1986.

The man and his nephew had been hunting from separate tree stands and by late afternoon, the witness was on his way to retrieve the younger man. The hunter was walking along a creek bottom that ran up to a swamp thicket when he noticed a terrible odor in the area. A few moments later, he heard what sounded like a man walking in the water. He thought it was his nephew coming to find him, so he called out to the young man. The hunter didn't get the expected response, however. The unseen figure quickly began moving away from the hunter's position. He recounts what happened next:

"Down the thicket about 50 to 75 yards there was a little opening about 30 feet across; this thing crossed the opening. I could not believe what I was seeing; this thing was around 6 to 7 feet tall with dark brown hair covering its whole body. It crossed the opening in what seemed to be 5 or 6 steps!" (BFRO).

The witness added that there was a "very foul smell" coming from the creature. He estimated that it weighed between 350 to 400 pounds, and it walked with a slight stoop.

The hunter retrieved his nephew and the two of them left the area immediately.

The sighting occurred at about 5:15 and the hunter had a good view of the creature. The area was at the edge of Wright Patman Lake, a body of water fed by the Sulphur River.

A man out deer hunting in Harrison County spotted a Bigfoot in the fall of 1987.

The man says he was standing on the shore of a lake watching the water when he caught movement out of the corner of his eye. Looking to his left, he saw a large creature come out of the water. It stood up, looked both ways, then walked off into the woods.

An investigator with the BFRO learned that the man was concealed at the edge of the water on the "southeast side of Benton Lake off Big Cypress Bayou above Caddo Lake."

The witness described the creature as being around six feet in height, black in color and covered with hair from head to toe.

I spoke to a man who told me he'd seen a Bigfoot on the banks of the Pedernales in the fall of 1989. The man was out for a day of canoeing and was moving at a slow pace, enjoying his outing. He was paddling slowly and occasionally stopped to look at birds or other wildlife in the area. As he was scanning the area, he noticed something odd on the riverbank to his right. He reports:

"It was crouching behind some bushes and as soon as I looked directly at it, it stood up. It was a good 6 ½ to 7 feet. I think it was curious about me I guess because I was in a canoe. It looked at me for a minute, then turned completely around and went back into the bushes. I'm sure it walked completely away from the area but even if it had left, I wasn't about to get out and go looking for it."

The man says the creature was covered in black hair and had very long, "ape-like arms" that hung to its knees. It stood on two legs and moved like a man. The witness is adamant that it wasn't a bear and he's sure it was not a hunter in a ghillie suit.

"The hair was close to the body, not shaggy. When it stood up, I could see its muscles flexing."

1990s

A group out fishing at Lake Ray Roberts in north Texas in 1990 had a strange encounter that began with the feeling that they were being watched by something. The unsettling feeling of being watched was followed by a loud screeching, then the sound of something barreling through the nearby tree line.

The group was armed, and they braced themselves for whatever was coming out of the woods. They started scanning the area with their flashlights and one of the lights illuminated the source of the disturbance—an eight-foot tall, bipedal creature. The thing was standing nearby and at first, it had its back to the men. The creature turned and started moving toward the group and one of the men opened fire with a shotgun. Reportedly, the man hit the creature dead center in its chest which caused the beast to let out a loud roar. The thing didn't go down, however. It pushed over a cottonwood tree and ran off into the woods. The creature was not seen by the group again.

Ray Crowe included the incident in his book *Bigfoot Behavior Volume I* and notes that the men reported that the cottonwood tree the thing pushed down was over eight inches in diameter and not a sapling.

Lake Ray Roberts

Ray Crowe's Western Bigfoot Society received a brief report involving a man hunting in east Texas in 1991. The hunter shot a deer and watched as a Bigfoot snatched it up and took off. The man and his father pursued the creature, tracking it by the trail of blood, but they were soon frightened off by threatening noises.

The TBRC (Texas Bigfoot Research Center) received a report from a woman who saw a creature cross the road near Pecan Gap in Fannin County in February 1992.

The woman was driving after midnight and had her high beams on. She spotted a large bipedal figure at the edge of her lights when it ran across the road ahead of her vehicle.

She told an investigator that the creature never turned toward her, so she saw it only in profile. It was seven foot or more in height and covered in very dark hair. The hair on the head was long and blended into the neck and shoulders. It was lean in build, and it swung its arms as it moved, traveling much faster than a man would.

The witness notes that she has heard screams at night in the area but always believed that the sounds were from panthers. She also reports that her father had heard stories of some kind of large creature in the area when he was growing up.

The sighting took place in a rural spot about a mile north of the North Sulphur River and a ½ mile to 1 mile from the nearest residence.

In October 1995 a man was out looking at a piece of property in Cleveland in Liberty County when he stumbled across a creature lying on the ground. The thing stood up on two legs, ran at the man, and hit him in the chest. The witness was able to capture some video of the creature, which was later broadcast on *Strange Universe*, a syndicated show that ran from 1996 to 1998. The authenticity of the footage is of course debated.

I received a report from a Newton County man who told me he'd seen a Bigfoot near his property in December 1995.

The creature was over six feet in height, covered in "long, dirty gray hair" and walked with a pronounced swinging of its arms. The witness was driving when he spotted the creature walking on the right side of the road. He reports:

"It was facing away from me, going the same direction I was driving. I slowed my truck way down trying to figure out what it was—it was some kind of man-animal, not like a gorilla, it stood more upright. It must have heard my truck cause all of a sudden it turned around and gave me an angry look, then stepped off into the trees."

The man got out, walked around to the front of his truck, and looked toward the spot where the creature had vanished. He didn't see it, but a "piercing scream" rang out and sent chills up his spine. He jumped back in his vehicle and left the area.

The witness added that the creature's face was "leathery" and the head was slightly pointed.

Ray Crowe mentions a brief report from 1996 involving a family in west Texas near the town of Big Spring in Howard County. The family was shocked when they spotted an eight-foot-tall creature staring through their kitchen window. Dogs all around the town were riled up and barking that night, waking many residents (Crowe, *Bigfoot Behavior Volume II*).

A seismographic surveyor working in Victoria County in June 1996 saw a large creature, 7 ½ to 8 feet in height. The man and an assistant were working in an area that had recently been cleared by a bulldozer. The witness says he looked up and saw a creature 125-150 feet away from his position. The thing walked out of the brush and stepped into the open where it stood for a moment. It looked at the men, then raised its nose as if it were trying to catch a scent. After a few seconds, the creature continued moving and vanished into the woods.

The two men went over to the area and saw the creature's prints. They were about eighteen inches in length and there were only four toes on each foot.

The witness described the creature as:

"About 7 ½ to 8 foot tall. Its knuckles nearly drug the ground, well, not really drug the ground, but they hung really low, below the knee area, and it was kind of stooped over. It was a light brown in color" (GCBRO).

The man also noted that even though the creature looked at the men, it didn't seem to care about their presence. The location of the sighting was near Goliad and about five miles away from the San Antonio River.

A police officer out on an ATV in San Jacinto County spotted a Bigfoot in August 1996.

The witness and a friend were riding on a straight, wide trail in the Sam Houston National Forest. The man turned to say something to his passenger and when he turned back around, he saw a creature in front of them. He described the beast as:

"A large humanoid creature, approximately 6-6.5 foot tall, broad shouldered and thick in appearance, with either dark brown or black hair covering its entire body. It spooked me and I yelled at my passenger to look. When I yelled the creature turned and ran into the woods" (BFRO).

The creature was 40-50 yards ahead of the vehicle when seen and the driver sped up to reach the spot where it vanished into the trees. He reports that tree limbs and brush were still shaking when he reached the area, but the creature was gone.

A man hunting in Delta County on December 15, 1996, had a startling daytime sighting of a Bigfoot.

The witness was hunting deer near the Sulphur River and was sitting in a position near a field full of cattle. Having hunted the area many times, he settled into his regular spot and waited, sitting there all morning. Suddenly the cattle on the other side of the pasture were alarmed by something that caused them to rush to the middle of the field. The hunter directed his attention to the area to see what had frightened the animals. He was stunned to observe a large, bipedal creature between 8 ½ to 9 feet in height walking along the far fence line. The witness notes that the six-strand barbwire fence only went to the creature's thigh/butt area.

The creature was solid black in color and the witness was surprised at the amount of ground it covered with its strides. The thing stopped twice and looked in the hunter's direction, causing the man to get an "ice cold feeling."

The sighting occurred between 11:30-11:45 under clear conditions. The man was sitting at the edge of a pasture and the property is all thicket and river bottoms at the north end of the Old Sulphur River.

In a follow-up report from the BFRO, the man notes that the creature's hair was short and had a "bluish gray cast." He also reported that the thing's shoulders were wide as if it were wearing "football shoulder pads."

The man also states: "Once in a while at night my wife and myself would hear a low bellow followed by a glass breaking shrill. [And a] loud growl. We lived 2 ½ or 3 miles from the North Sulphur River."

A man working on a pipeline in Victoria County spotted a Bigfoot the last weekend of November 1997.

The man and a helper were near the town of Goliad around 9:30 in the evening when they saw a large, hairy creature walking nearby. The thing was about eight feet in height, light brown in color, had long arms, and walked on two legs.

The two men were shocked at the sight and quickly loaded up their gear and left the area.

The man decided he wanted to investigate the area so the following morning he went out early and went into the woods where he'd seen the creature. The man's helper refused to even get out of the truck, so the reporting witness entered the woods on his own. As he was exploring, the man came across a strange and disturbing sight. He reports:

"I entered the woods and was only a couple of hundred yards from where we saw it the night before and came upon something that struck me as odd. There in the middle of the woods were 5 dead deer all stacked into a pile. I could not for the life of me figure out why there were 5 dead deer placed into a pile in such a fashion" (GCBRO).

An account detailed by Ray Crowe in his book *Bigfoot Behavior Volume III* involves a man named Ken who was traveling outside of Mount Enterprise through the Piney Woods of east

Texas on January 11, 1998. Ken was headed east on Highway 84 around 11:30 that evening when his high beams caught a large black figure on the side of the road. The man slowed his truck down in order to observe the figure. The thing was on the ground rolling around "like it was trying to scratch."

Seeing the truck, the creature stood up on two legs and began walking toward the vehicle on the left side of the road. It then stood next to the road, jumping up and down and beating its chest like an ape.

At first, the witness thought the figure might be a man in an ape suit, but as he watched closely, he realized it was something else. He says the thing was very large in size and did not retreat from the area. The creature was black in color, broad in stature, and between 6 ½ to 7 feet in height. Its eyes were reflective, further indicating that it was not merely a man in a costume.

The location of the sighting was east of Mount Enterprise in an area of heavy woods, brush, and swamp.

In November 1998, a pair of hunters spotted a Bigfoot near Longview in Gregg County. One of the hunters fired three shots at the creature. It made a grunting sound and the hunters thought that it had been hit but the grunt was followed by a loud roar that sent the men running through the woods for the safety of a house. They described the creature as eight feet in height and covered with hair (Crowe, *Bigfoot Behavior Volume I*).

Also, in November that same year, another pair of hunters in Anderson County saw a large creature, about six feet in height, running bipedally "around the speed of a deer."

The reporting witness told the GCBRO that the creature was covered in long gray hair. It jumped over a fence and vanished into the woods.

A man bowfishing for gar in Newton County saw a Bigfoot in April 1999. A BFRO investigator spoke with the man and got details of the encounter.

The man was on a boat on the Sabine River Bottoms between 1 p.m. and 3 p.m. On the nearby bank, about thirty yards away, he saw a creature over six feet in height and covered with hair. Initially, the creature was turned away from the man, so he didn't see its face.

The fisherman slowly put his bow down. In doing so, he accidentally made a slight noise when the bow touched the bottom of the aluminum boat. Alerted by the sound, the creature turned, looked at the man, and emitted a "high-pitched scream like a woman"; after screaming it turned and began walking away.

The witness grabbed his paddle and slapped the water, causing the creature to exit the area more rapidly.

The witness was an ex-military man and made a number of observations about the thing he saw. He says the creature was covered with reddish-brown hair, had dark colored skin on its face and palms and had a "monkey-like face." The nose was flat, and the teeth were sharper than a human's teeth.

Curiously, he also noted that the creature's eyes seemed to have a golden glow or tint to them.

The man admitted that he had previously heard "screams" and "whoops" while hunting along the river. He had heard other people talk about the existence of the creatures in the area, though until his own encounter, he had always been skeptical of the accounts.

2000s

A report on the *Bigfoot Encounters* website details an August 5, 2001, encounter in Anderson County.

The reporting witness was traveling on Highway 287 and was thirty-one miles west of the town of Palestine. At 3:31 a.m., the driver slowed down because of a large animal in the road ahead. He switched on his high beams and turned on his four-way flashers along with an interior spotlight. The man recounts what he saw:

"As I looked up, I saw a huge bipedal creature that I will call Bigfoot. It walked from the soft shoulder of the road to the animal in the road. As he (I am pretty sure it was a male) walked in front of my tractor he shielded his eyes, not seemingly out of shyness, but more as an effort to protect his eyes from the bright lights. I reduced my headlights to low beams, but decided not to turn them off as I was in the middle of the highway. I was doing my best to protect them by blocking the road with my tractor-trailer. The big male went over to what I realized was a 'toddler.'"

What ensued next was a scuffle similar to that between a human parent and a child. The man says that the large creature tried to take the smaller one's arm, but the smaller creature retreated away clearly not wanting to go. The witness says the small creature "squirmed, scrambled, and scooted further up the road" in an effort to elude its parent. As the man sat watching the creatures, he noticed movement next to the driver's side of his vehicle. Looking in the direction of the movement, the man spotted a female creature. He reports:

"Her eyes were almost even with my eye level. I measured from where the top of her head came up to my mirror; it was 7' 4" tall. The male was at least one foot taller than her, plus some. She had a 'gamy' smell but didn't stink."

The man smiled at the creature and asked: "Is the baby okay?" He says the female creature slowly "smiled" back at him. At that point, he noticed a dental anomaly that implied that the creature had a double row of teeth. The creature then reached inside the vehicle and stroked the man's beard.

"I extended my hand out to her. She sandwiched my hand between her two hands; her hands were 2X-3X larger than mine. Her hands felt like roughneck work gloves (rough leather). At this point she gave me a 'soulful' look. From her facial expressions and watery eyes, I took it that she was saying, 'Thanks for not running over my baby.' The eyes were not dead eyes, they were bright and moist, just very dark brown, not black."

The witness says the female was covered with hair/fur that was reddish-brown in color while the male's hair was dark brown with traces of gray/white on its shoulders, back and chest.

The male Bigfoot swept up the small creature and carried it under his arm "like a sack of potatoes." The male never looked over at the driver during the entire incident.

The man says there were at least three more creatures in the treeline, though he did not see them clearly.

In December 2001 a deer hunter out near Marshall in Harrison County saw a seven-foot-tall ape-like creature. The thing was dark brown in color, stood on two legs, and was somewhat stooped in its posture. The hunter had put apples out to attract deer and had instead attracted a Bigfoot. The creature picked the apples up and left the area. Apparently, the thing was preparing a feast since it was also carrying the hindquarter of a deer when it was spotted (Bord, *Bigfoot Casebook*).

A Bigfoot was spotted near Paris, Texas

In the truth or fiction category comes a report received by the Texas Bigfoot Research Center about an incident near the town of Paris in Lamar County.

Purportedly, a man out checking his hog traps on July 19, 2002, discovered that he had snared something other than a hog;

he had caught a juvenile Bigfoot.

According to the report, the creature was four feet tall, had black hair, small hands and feet. and a face like a gorilla. Purportedly, the little creature was very worked up and banging against the cage, clearly wanting out. The witness says he released the creature.

Various tracks were also found in the area and measured from nine inches up to eighteen inches in length.

In 2003 a motorist traveling on Texas Highway 154 in Harleton, Harrison County, saw an eight-foot-tall creature near Little Cypress Bayou (Dallas/Fort Worth *Star-Telegram*, October 10, 2004).

Strange things were afoot in the Trinity area of Houston County on December 15, 2003. Horses in the area were spooked by something unseen and neighborhood dogs were anxiously barking. Residents said there were terrible screams echoing around the area and people heard odd "wood clicking" sounds.

A report on the incident posted on the *Oregon Bigfoot* site came from a man in the area who reported that something had visited a deer feeder he had out and taken the corn. "I saw where this animal climbed up the ravine and ate the deer corn," he stated.

Ray Crowe mentions an incident that took place near El Campo in Wharton County in September 2004. A woman was sitting on her porch around ten o'clock at night when she heard a strange noise, a sound she said resembled something heavy stepping on a sheet of tin that was lying on the ground. The frightened woman called out for her husband who was inside the home. When the man opened the door, the couple's pit bull rushed inside the house in a state of fear. The couple soon saw the source of the dog's panic. Crowe reports:

"Suddenly, this grayish creature, looking like an overgrown monkey, jumped up on the corner of a refrigerator that was nearby. Her husband fired the pistol, and it ran off very fast as he did" (Crowe, *Bigfoot Behavior Vol II*).

On January 6, 2005, at 1:30 a.m., Amos Washington was

driving his 18-wheeler north of Interstate 10 through Hudspeth County when something ran across the road in front of his rig.

"I don't know for sure what I seen. The sight of this thing challenged anything I know about—it wasn't something a person can imagine. It was slumped some, naked, hair-covered, and light brown to white on its shoulders."

At the time of his sighting, Washington says he was east of Fort Bliss and about three miles out of the town of Butterfield on Highway 62. He says the creature was barefoot and had long legs. He didn't notice any other features and in moments, the creature had disappeared into the darkness.

The BFRO has a pair of sightings from 2011 that took place near the town of Aledo in Parker County. Both sightings occurred around a gas well site and were reported by men working at the locations.

The first incident, from June, involved a man who was working late at night at a site with six gas tanks. The tanks, it's noted, had loud compressors. It was around 2 a.m. and the man was connecting hoses when he noticed eyeshine from the woods behind the site. The man had a head lamp on his hard hat, and he directed the beam toward the spot to try to see what kind of animal was there. What he saw wasn't any ordinary animal, however, but a large, bipedal creature.

The man told investigator Gary Christensen that the thing was between 7 ½ to 8 feet in height and muscular in shape. He also noted "a short but visible neck, short hair, [and] a pupil in the reflective eyes."

The man is a hunter and is very familiar with local wildlife. When he spotted the creature, he ran to his truck and phoned his boss to report the incident. His boss, a longtime resident of the area, reportedly stated that many locals had reported stories of such a "monster" in the area.

The reporting witness stated: "I am not scared of a man, but that was not a man."

A truck driver was the second person to report an encounter from the area. On the night of August 26th, the man was at the gas site when he too spotted eyeshine in the area. Right after this, something started throwing rocks at a tank not far from where the witness was standing. The man reports:

"The first thing that caught my attention was the lack of wildlife sounds and the smell of a skunk, and the sound of something that sounded like a growl. Another person had put a game camera up, and it got a picture of something blocking the camera 30 min before I had got there. I have seen other things in my time as a truck driver, but this is a little too close to home."

When Gary Christensen followed up on the report, he examined the photograph caught by the game camera. He reports that "it shows a 9/10 black exposure with no detail." The interesting thing about the photograph, Christensen notes, is the timing of something blocking the camera shortly before the man's encounter.

Christensen also learned that the rocks that were being thrown were about the size of tennis balls and likely came from the nearby riverbed. The witness told Christensen that even though the rocks didn't land near him or his vehicle, he still felt intimidated.

Intriguingly, the witness also reported that others at the site were aware that some large creature was in the area, and at least one individual was visibly shaken by an event at the site that he wouldn't discuss.

KLTV7, East Texas, reported on Bigfoot sightings on October 22, 2012, noting that reports had come from areas as diverse as Dallas to remote portions in the eastern part of the state.

The news included claims from an anonymous Dallas photographer who said that he had encountered a "family group" of Bigfoot who got as close as fifteen feet from him. "There was one about 10 foot tall," he proclaimed, "It looked like something out of a Steven Spielberg movie, not human as I know it."

The images and videos appear to show *something* large watching from the trees, but some researchers feel the pics are simply another example of an infamous "blobsquatch," an undefined blur that is most likely matrixing or something natural in the environment.

As for the photographer, he reports that he has captured images in Shelby County and in another area outside of Dallas. He told *KLTV7* that he would be releasing more of his evidence in the future.

A witness in the Sudan area of Lamb County encountered a creature on July 7, 2013. Ray Crowe included the report in his *Bigfoot Behavior Vol II*. The reporting witness noticed a tree near the road that had tumbleweed all around it, piled up to where the limbs began. The tumbleweeds appeared to be placed intentionally as if being used to conceal something. The witness states:

"I noticed the tumbleweeds were a muddy tan color like they had dried mud on them. I saw that they were that way because there was something dark sitting there facing towards the draw away from the road."

The witness says the figure was a "dark hairy creature" that kept "moving around the tree to make it look like there was nothing there."

A man driving in Van Zandt County on October 30, 2015, was startled to see a Bigfoot along the road at 3 o'clock in the morning.

The man was driving below the speed limit, being cautious of wildlife in the area. He was crossing a bridge on FM 279 when his headlights caught something unexpected, a "big hairy thing carrying a deer."

The witness told BFRO investigator Paul Ragsdale that the creature was between 8 and 9 feet in height and was carrying the deer over its left shoulder.

The creature's head was conical in shape, and it appeared to have no neck. It was covered with "reddish black" hair and the witness saw white/yellow eye shine. Ragsdale spoke to the witness a couple of years after the sighting and the man was still shaken about the incident, noting that he still couldn't get the thing's "glowing eyes" out of his head.

While the creature did turn to look at the approaching vehicle, it continued moving and soon disappeared into the thick woods. The witness estimated that the entire sighting lasted about 5-10 seconds. He said the Bigfoot was about ten yards away as it moved into the tree line on the side of the road.

Bigfoot Through the Decades

PART THREE
Strange Things in the Texas Sky

Weird Things Above

With its wide-open skies, it comes as no surprise that Texas is home to numerous reports of strange things flying through the air. As we shall see here, sightings run the gamut from large, prehistoric-looking creatures to giant birds and even winged humanoids.

The state does have a wide and diverse range of bird species. According to the official state bird list, there are 663 species in Texas. The list includes 169 birds designated as "review species" meaning there are confirmed sightings in Texas but not official recognition that the species is living in the state.

It's also notable that fossils of the Quetzalocatlus were discovered in Big Bend National Park in 1972. The prehistoric monster was a pterosaur that had a wingspan between thirty and forty feet. A massive creature indeed and although long extinct, it's curious in conjunction with some of the reported sightings of prehistoric looking birds in the state.

Of course, there are always those weird, historic accounts of creatures that sound incredible. Take the report from June 1873 about a farmer named Hardin.

The man was out with several of his field hands when they saw an "enormous serpent" in the sky. The men were working on a farm in Bonham in Fannin County when they spotted the creature. According to the report:

"They said that the yellow striped creature was about the same length and width as a telephone pole and that it undulated toward the eastern sky using much the same type of movement as would an ordinary snake." (Note this report is from an old news clipping with no original source listed.)

There's folklore about giant winged creatures in the state

as well, the best known of which is the Mexican legend of "La Lechuza."

La Lechuza reportedly stands up to seven feet in height and has a wingspan of fifteen feet or more. The giant, winged creature is said to resemble an oversized owl or raven, can be black or white in color, and has the face of an old woman.

La Lechuza has supernatural elements as well. It's said to be a vengeful spirit that feeds on negative emotions and it's known to kidnap and eat children.

Being rooted in Mexican folklore, it's no surprise that stories of La Lechuza are especially prominent along the Texas/ Mexico border.

The creature is said to frequently show up in the guise of a giant owl, and there's no doubt that sightings of large owls were probably terrifying for some people who had the legend of La Lechuza in mind.

With the creature's propensity for snatching up children and taking them away, it has, in some cases, fulfilled the classic boogey-man role to keep youngsters in line.

Still, the lore surrounding the winged monster is not so simple or straightforward. Some legends identify La Lechuza as a witch who can shapeshift into its winged form, owl-like but still with a human face. Such creatures are reportedly witches who made a deal with the devil in order to gain magical powers.

In some lore, when the La Lechuza chooses a victim, it perches in the distance and starts making whistling sounds or the sounds of a baby to attract the victim's attention. When the person goes to investigate, they are snapped up by the giant owl and carried off to be devoured.

Despite the connections to witches, the devil and the supernatural, there are still people in modern times that believe in the existence of La Lechuza and some even claim to have encountered the thing.

A woman named Rosa told me that she saw one when she was a teenager in 1972. She said the creature was lurking outside her family's home along the Texas/Mexico border. She described it as six feet in height with large, black wings and the face of a "wrinkled old woman."

Rosa's sighting was brief and, while frightening for her at the time, it was mostly uneventful since the creature didn't attack or harass her in any way. Did she merely see a large owl, or was it something else?

Another report passed on to me comes from 1977 and involves a woman in Santa Rosa, Cameron County, who said she saw a giant bird creature with black eyes and a face like an old woman. The bird was in a tree and flew down straight at the woman as if to attack. The woman fled into her house but once inside, the bird started scratching against the door as if trying to get into the home. Shades of Alfred Hitchcock!

The bird finally retreated when some neighborhood dogs showed up and gave chase, pursuing it until they were all out of sight. Adding to the creepiness of the story, the following day when the dogs had failed to return, searchers discovered their mangled bodies in the woods. The poor animals had been torn apart and mutilated by something powerful.

LONE STAR STATE MONSTERS by David Weatherly

The Houston Batman

June 18, 1953, was another hot day in Houston. Air conditioning wasn't common at the time and residents did whatever they could for relief from the summer heat. Even so, there were many restless nights for people who simply found it too hot and humid to rest. Such was the case for some residents in the historic Heights neighborhood.

At 2:30 a.m., Hilda Walker, a 23-year-old housewife, was sitting outside talking to two of her neighbors—14-year-old Judy Myers and 33-year-old Howard Phillips, a tool plant inspector. The trio were outside an apartment building on East Third Street and likely didn't expect anything more than continued humidity that night. The normalcy of the night was disrupted when Hilda spotted something unusual about twenty-five feet from the group's position.

Walker said she saw a "huge shadow across the lawn." She focused on the object, trying to discern exactly what she was seeing.

"I thought at first it was the magnified reflection of a big moth caught in a nearby streetlight. Then the shadow seemed to bounce upward into a pecan tree," she reported (*Fate* magazine, October 1953).

She pointed the anomaly out to her friends who also saw the figure and they all watched as it came into focus. They were looking at a humanoid figure with wings like those of a bat. The winged man was dressed in black or grey tight-fitting clothing. He perched silently on the branch of the pecan tree.

According to the witnesses, the man was about six and a half feet tall and was clad in skin-tight pants, quarter length boots, and a black cape. Mrs. Walker added: "I could see him plain and could see he had big wings folded at his shoulders."

One of the other witnesses added that the strange man "was dressed in a uniform like a paratrooper wears."

Adding to the weirdness of the sighting, the winged figure was encased in a "halo of light."

The weird figure sat on the pecan branch, rocking back and forth, for about thirty seconds. Then, the light surrounding it began to fade and the figure disappeared. When it did, Judy let out a scream.

A short time after the sighting, there was a loud whooshing sound on the other side of the street and the witnesses saw a torpedo-shaped flash of light shoot up into the air at tremendous speed.

Hilda was so disturbed by the encounter that she phoned the police the following day and reported the incident.

Reporters got word of the story and the *Houston Chronicle* covered the incident. Given the time period of the sighting, and the interest in flying saucers, some people speculated that there was a connection between the Batman and UFOs.

When he was talking to reporters about the event, Howard Phillips even referenced the topic:

"I've heard so much about flying saucer stories and I thought all those people telling the stories were crazy, but now I don't know what to believe. I saw it, whatever it was."

LONE STAR STATE MONSTERS by David Weatherly

Winged Oddities of '70s

The Batman may have been gone, but in the coming years, plenty of other winged oddities showed up in the state, especially in the 1970s. While the record of accounts from the 1960s is slim, there's one that's notable in light of what was to come in the 70s.

In August 1966 a man named Tony and his fiancé Maria were sitting in a vehicle outside of Tony's mother's home in San Benito, Cameron County. At 1 a.m., the pair spotted a weird creature perched on a telephone pole near their vehicle.

According to the witnesses, the creature was a bird but larger than a man. It was black in color and about a yard in width. Its wings were large and folded around its body. Chillingly, the creature stayed perched on the pole staring directly at the couple. They fled inside the house to get away from the thing (Clark and Coleman, *Creatures from the Goblin World*).

The August 1976 edition of the *Ohio Skywatcher* included a 1971 sighting from San Antonio reported by Annie Rosenbloom and John Michael. The report states:

"Two witnesses spotted a creature resembling a 'pterosaur'—resembling a flying dragon. Reportedly had a wingspan of 20 feet, big bony wings, no feathers, leathery dry skin stretched across big bony flexing fingers. Made big droopy loops in the air and at same time [issued] an eerie guttural scream. Moved about blindly like a huge bat, then moved off to the mountains."

Writing in the 1976 edition of *Saga UFO Annual*, Jerome Clark reported on bizarre incidents from the Spring of 1975 that took place near the town of Henderson in Rusk County.

A farmer out gathering hay bales with his pickup truck was

alerted to the sound of a dog barking in alarm on the opposite side of a nearby rise. He drove over to the area to see what had the animal excited. When he got over the rise, he saw a black, man-like creature emerging from the pine trees. The creature was winged, and it suddenly took to the air, flying up to a black helicopter that was hovering overhead. The winged being went inside the chopper and the craft left the area.

Clark notes that the farmer had seen the helicopter a few days before and had also discovered the remains of a mutilated cow in the area.

1976 turned out to be a banner year for giant flying creatures in the Lone Star State. The creature, or creatures, that showed up during the flap are often referred to as the "Big Bird," or "Bird Man." Reports were especially prevalent in the Rio Grande Valley region during this period.

Some people thought the thing was simply a giant bird, perhaps of some unknown species, while others thought it was something prehistoric. Still other accounts indicate something even more bizarre—a bird-like humanoid with some human-like or ape-like features. Many reports indicate that the thing was terrifying with a long beak, claws, and glowing eyes. Whatever the thing was, a lot of people reported seeing it.

Even years after the events, people have continued to come forward and report their sightings of giant birds in the region.

Ken Gerhard has studied accounts of giant winged creatures in Texas extensively. In his book *Menagerie of Mysterious Beasts*, he relates an account he received from a Texas resident named Fiona who recalled seeing a dinosaur-like bird in 1976. She writes:

"Both my ex-husband and I saw a giant bird over Houston, Texas, in '76. It was quite close and looked like a pterodactyl. I'll never forget the huge size of it, the enormous wingspan, the clearly defined point at the back of the skull, and the long legs trailing behind. It wasn't just gliding, it was smoothly flapping its wings. I saw it as I was looking out the patio door and called my husband to come take a look. He saw it too and tried to call a radio or TV station, but they wouldn't believe him."

Fiona notes that for the longest time, she wasn't aware that other people in the state had seen anything similar. When she happened to catch a documentary on television about the big bird sightings in Texas during the 1970s, she was relieved. She told Gerhard:

"It was gratifying to find out that others had seen the giants as well. The skeptics try to say it was a giant condor or something like that. It wasn't. You could clearly see the long, slim neck, pointed beak, pointed skull, and long, slim legs. I think of it as my UFOs, as I now know what it feels like to try and tell others of something that sounds impossible and they don't believe you."

A ten-year-old boy saw a large, bird-like creature in Houston one night in January 1976. The young man was outside at the time and there was a thunderstorm in the area.

According to the report on the now defunct *UFOsabout.com*, the winged creature was about eight feet tall, had a twenty-foot wingspan and red, glowing eyes. The creature landed about six feet from the boy, causing him to freeze in place out of fear. The boy's dog suddenly ran forward, barking and running toward the winged thing. The dog's barking spurred the boy into action. He jumped on top of his father's car and began screaming for help. The boy's father rushed outside to see what was wrong. Amidst the flurry, the creature flew away. The father discovered "strange prints" where the thing had been standing.

On January 1, 1976, eleven-year-old Tracey Lawson was playing outside in the backyard of her home in Harlingen, in Cameron County, with her fourteen-year-old cousin, Jackie Davies.

The two girls noticed something strange near a pit bordering an irrigation canal about 100 yards from their position. Tracey retrieved a pair of field binoculars from inside and the girls used the glasses to get a better look at the creature. They saw a "horrible looking" black bird over five feet in height. The ugly looking creature had a gorilla-like face, bald head, and large, luminous red eyes. The beak, they reported, was at least six inches long.

The girls said that the thing glared at them for a while, then let out a terrible shriek and vanished behind some trees. Moments later, the thing reappeared at the northeast corner of the property, poking its head up over a small cluster of trees.

The girls reported the creature to their parents, but the adults dismissed the story—until the next day, that is. Jackie's stepfather, Tom Waldon, discovered weird, three-toed tracks in the area where the girls said the bird thing had been lurking. The tracks measured eight inches across and were unlike anything Waldon had seen before. They were pressed an inch and a half into the hard packed ground. It was also reported that the Lawson family dog, a normally friendly and energetic animal, began to act very strangely around this time. The dog refused to go outside and would hide in its doghouse as if it were afraid of something. At suppertime, the dog bolted into the house and had to be dragged back outside.

Later that night, Mr. Lawson heard what sounded like large wings scraping on his bedroom window, but whatever it was left no evidence of its visit.

In the early morning hours of January 3, 1976, two San Benito police officers had an encounter with an unusual, winged creature while they were on patrol.

Officers Arturo Padilla and Homero Galvan reported seeing a massive bird that swept down over their patrol cars. They said the bird had a huge wingspan and a long neck that was curled up into an S shape as it flew by.

Padilla first spotted the creature in the headlights of his cruiser. A few moments later, Homer Galvan spotted the thing in the same area. Galvan said the creature looked like a large black silhouette gliding through the air and noted that he never saw it flap its wings.

Local wildlife experts asserted that the officers had seen a normal bird, namely a pelican, but Padilla, a seasoned hunter, stated that while the creature did look like a bird to him, it had a wingspan of about fifteen feet, well beyond the wingspan of even the largest pelicans.

On January 7, 1976, a man named Alverico Guajardo was

eating dinner in his mobile home just outside of the town of Brownsville in Cameron County.

It was around 9:30 at night when he heard something strike the trailer with a loud thud. Worried about the safety of his family, Guajardo grabbed a pocketknife and rushed outside ready to confront whoever, or whatever, was causing trouble. In the darkness, he saw the silhouette of a large animal on the ground near his home. With no flashlight at hand, the man got in his station wagon and turned on the headlights to illuminate the object.

The glare of the headlights shining on the creature caused it to react and it rose quickly, looking at Alverico with eyes the size of silver dollars and blazing red in color.

The man later told reporters with the local paper: "I was scared. It's got wings like a bird, but it's not a bird. That animal is not from this world" (*Brownsville Herald*, January 9, 1976).

Guajardo reported that the creature made a horrible noise. Although the bird's beak didn't move, its neck pulsed, and the sound seemed to issue from deep in its throat.

The beast was about four feet in height with black feathers and a beak 2-4 feet in length. The thing's wings were bat-like and folded around its shoulders. After it issued the strange noise, the bird started backing up toward the dirt road several feet away, doing so until it vanished in the darkness.

Jerome Clark notes in his book *Unexplained* that a pair of ranch hands south of San Antonio saw a five-foot-tall bird-like creature standing in a water stock tank on the night of January 11, 1976.

While the men were observing it, the thing took to the air. One of the witnesses, Jessie Garcia, stated: "He started flying but I never saw him flap his wings. He made no noise at all."

On the afternoon of January 12, 1976, sisters Libby and Deany Ford saw a "big black bird" near a pond northeast of Brownsville. Libby reported that the creature had a "face like a bat." When the girls later looked through a book to identify the creature, they said it looked like a pterodactyl (Clark,

Unexplained).

On the evening of January 14, 1976, Armando Grimaldo was standing outside of his mother-in-law's home north of Raymondville in Willacy County smoking a cigarette.

Armando heard what sounded like the flapping of bat wings and an odd whistling sound. At the same time, dogs around the neighborhood started barking, clearly alarmed by something. Grimaldo looked around for the source of the disturbance but didn't see anything unusual from where he was standing. He turned to go and look around the other side of the home when something attacked him. Grimaldo felt large claws tearing at him. He looked back and saw his attacker as he was running away to escape the assault: it was a giant bird.

The sound of Grimaldo's screaming brought neighbors outside, but by the time they made it to him, the bird was gone.

Grimaldo was later treated for minor scratches and shock at Willacy County Hospital, and he remained bedridden for two days after the incident. Newspapers quickly reported on the attack:

"The bird reportedly tore Grimaldo's shirt off and ripped his pants. A spokesman for the Willacy County sheriff's office said Grimaldo told them a big black bird with big eyes and a monkey-like face attacked him" (*Corpus Christi Caller-Times*, January 16, 1976).

Janet and Colin Bord's book, *Alien Animals*, notes two incidents from January 18, 1976. The first came from a man driving near Olmito in Cameron County. The man saw a bizarre, winged creature he said had a twelve-foot wingspan. The thing was between four and five feet tall and had a face that resembled a monkey or a cat.

The Bords also note a report from Homer and Marie Hernandez who reported seeing a giant bird, about four feet in height with a 4-6-inch-long beak. The bird was at an irrigation canal in San Benito in Cameron County. While the couple thought the animal was odd, it's likely they simply saw an unusual or out of place bird.

Another strange incident occurred on January 21, 1976, when a man named Francisco Magallanez was reportedly attacked by a giant birdman at a place called, fittingly, Eagle Pass in Maverick County.

Magallanez had stepped out into the backyard of his home when he spotted a large, winged creature that was stooped over near a clothesline. The creature made a loud hissing sound, then pounced on Francisco's shoulders. It ripped into the man with its talons, then hopped off. It's not clear from the reports whether the thing flew off or ran away. Magallanez may not have seen where the thing went, considering the attacks he suffered.

A doctor confirmed that the man did indeed have deep scratches that appeared to have been inflicted by some kind of wild animal, though it wasn't clear what had assaulted the man.

Magallanez told police officers that the thing had a dark brown body that was almost black in color, bright red eyes, and bat-like wings. He also reported that it had short, stubby legs and two arms that were around two and a half feet in length.

Adding to the bizarre description, the witness said the creature had pointed ears and the face of a pig—minus the snout. Unusual feathers were reportedly found at the scene of the attack, but no one was able to get to the bottom of the incident.

After the stories hit local newspapers, people became so worried that they were afraid to go outside at night, lest the birdman swoop down and attack.

Scattered reports and rumors of vanished pets and mutilated animals in the area added to the strange mix of tales and fear that were circulating in the region.

On February 24, 1976, a trio of teachers from San Antonio's Southside School District had a strange encounter while on their way to work.

The witnesses, David Rendon, Patricia Bryant, and Marsha Dahlberg, were driving in separate vehicles on an isolated road ten miles south of San Antonio when a large bird swooped down over their cars. The bird cast a massive shadow on the road and all three teachers pulled over in order to take a closer look at the thing. Once they had stopped and began observing the sky more closely, they realized that there were actually two winged creatures flying overhead. One of the creatures was circling over their vehicles while the other flew circles over a herd of cattle in a nearby field. The teachers observed the creatures closely, trying to discern what they were witnessing. Patricia Bryant told reporters:

"I could see the skeleton of this bird through the skin or feathers or whatever and it stood out black against the background of grey feathers. It was the biggest thing I've ever seen alive, particularly flying. It all happened so fast, and it was such a shock you think you are seeing things. It was enormous and frightening" (*Tyler Morning Telegraph*, March 2, 1976).

Artistic concept of an ancient flying creature

Both the female witnesses estimated that the birds were the size of a Piper Cub airplane. "This bird looks like it was half-reptile, half-bird. The wing had two joints in it like a chicken wing. I definitely saw it did have feathers," Bryant stated.

David Rendon reported that the creatures' wings were bony and leathery and that they didn't really fly but glided through the air.

After the incident, the teachers searched through reference books to try to identify the creatures they had seen. They all determined that it resembled a Pteranodon.

John S. Carroll was living on a pig farm in the unincorporated area of Montalba in Anderson County when he spotted a massive bird on December 8, 1976. Carroll said the bird was 8-foot-tall and had a 12-inch bill. The bird was standing in a pond on his property and was bluish, steel grey with a golden breast.

The animal took to the air, then landed in a tree nearby. Carroll thought the bird was after his pigs, so he fired at it. He saw the bird fall but when he investigated the spot, all he found were some bloody feathers (Bord, *Alien Animals*).

Less than ten days later, on December 17th, a similar bird was spotted in a field fifteen miles northwest of the Carroll property. The witness who saw the animal said that it had an injured wing. The same bird was reportedly spotted yet again on December 22, another three miles away at Catfish Creek.

While these sightings fell within the time frame of other "big bird" sightings in the region, it seems clear that Carroll took a shot at a regular living animal, likely a rare or out-of-place species and very possibly an endangered or protected one.

There was certainly a lot of excitement about all the big bird sightings in 1976 and the media attention did a lot to fuel the stories. After a television station showed an alleged photograph of the giant bird's track—one that measured twelve inches in length—the media hype grew.

A local radio station offered a reward for the capture of the creature, resulting in a horde of monster hunters showing up hoping to cash in on the critter.

Officials with the Texas Parks and Wildlife Department were concerned and worried about protected birds like the whooping crane being hurt or killed, especially with so many people running around with itchy trigger fingers hoping for easy cash. Wildlife officials put out an announcement emphasizing state and federal laws that protect bird species.

Indeed, there were some false alarms during the period, including a mass sighting of a large, winged creature flying around just south of Alamo, in Hidalgo County. The monster in this case turned out to be a blue heron.

Ken Gerhard recalls speaking with a man named Alex Resendez who said he'd seen giant birds twice in the 1970s.

The first incident occurred in Brownsville when he overheard talk of a giant bird on his C.B. radio. According to the report, the creature was on the roof of the Brownsville police station. Deciding to have a look for himself, Resendez went down to the station, and, sure enough, he spotted a large, shadowy form with wings perched on top of the building.

Resendez's second sighting of a giant bird was out in the country near the town of Edinburg in Hidalgo County. Alex was taking a nap when he was roused by his young son shouting about a big bird in the field. Resendez investigated and saw the creature standing in a nearby cow pasture about fifty yards away. He says it had a strange, transparent looking beak.

The man's son was so excited about the bird that before anyone could react, the boy jumped over the fence and into the pasture. Just after he did, the boy found himself facing an angry bull that began to charge him. Part way toward the child, the bull turned and went after the bird, causing it to take to the air.

Resendez says that when the bird took off, blue and white stripes were visible on its underside.

LONE STAR STATE MONSTERS by David Weatherly

More Giants & Flying Humanoids

Long after the flap of 1976, reports of strange things flying over Texas continued to crop up.

On September 14, 1982, an ambulance driver named James Thompson spotted a strange flying creature near Los Fresnos in Cameron County. Thompson was on his way back from an inspection on South Padre Island at the time of his sighting.

He first saw the bird-like creature flying low over the highway about 150 feet ahead of his vehicle. He hit the brakes and pulled over to observe the creature more closely. It was black to gray in color, had no feathers and had rough textured skin. The creature's wingspan was five to six feet and the wings had indentions on the tops and possibly the bottoms. The creature also had a hump "like a Brahma bull" on the back of its head and it had almost no neck. Thompson said the creature's body ended with a "fin" that stretched over eight feet.

Curious about what he had seen, the man later looked through some books and decided that the bird-like creature he'd spotted most closely resembled a pterosaur.

My colleague Nick Redfern reported on a flying humanoid in his book *The NASA Conspiracies: The Truth Behind the Moon Landings, Censored Photos, and the Face on Mars*.

The incident occurred in 1986 at NASA's Johnson Space Center in Houston and was reported by the witness's daughter. According to the woman, Desiree, her father arrived home from work one night in a distressed state and appeared on the verge of an anxiety attack. After Desiree and her mother were finally able to calm the man down, he revealed why he had been in such a panic.

The man recounted that he had left work and was walking

to his vehicle when he spotted a strange figure perched on a building nearby. The man-like shape was completely black in color and had what appeared to be a large cape draped across its shoulders and back. It also had what appeared to be wing-like appendages sticking out of the sides of the cape. The wings were more bat-like than bird-like, and they made a cracking noise as they slowly flapped in the strong, howling wind.

According to Desiree, her father reported that the creature realized that it had been spotted and the man had the distinct impression that the thing was pleased that it was being observed.

The witness was frozen to the spot and could only stand unmoving, staring at the thing in terror. After an undetermined amount of time, the man suddenly came to his senses, rushed to his vehicle, and fled the scene, rushing home as fast as he could.

For several weeks, the man kept quiet about his encounter, but he was so disturbed by the incident that he eventually confided in his superior at work. Surprisingly, the man admitted that the creature had been seen on other occasions wandering around the darker parts of the Space Center.

Redfern reports that a secret file had purportedly been opened to collect accounts of the creature. According to the file, the remains of two dead German shepherds had been found at the Space Center, in the same general location where Desiree's father had seen the thing perched. The bodies of the dogs had been horrifically mutilated, and a significant amount of the dog's blood had been drained.

After he revealed his sighting of the winged creature to his boss, Desiree's father was grilled by a pair of special NASA security people who had flown in from Arizona to speak with him.

A report on the *True Horror Stories of Texas* website involves an encounter from the Three Rivers area from 2000. The reporting witness was driving on I-37 between San Antonio and Corpus Christi at about 1 a.m. when he saw: "A large, white humanoid figure with wings. Not a crane, or goose, or swan, or bird of prey, but a humanoid figure with skin wings."

The driver reports that he was moving at around 65 mph

and the creature came from the right rear side of his car crossing at about a forty-five-degree angle. The creature was moving fast and overtook the driver's speed by 5-10 mph. The witness continued:

"As it crossed over me it was only 10 or so feet above the roof of my vehicle. [The] wingspan was probably 6-8 feet, and the skin was white. The wings looked to be constructed/shaped more like you would expect to see on a bat or pterodactyl but with solidly defined human arms on the leading edge. There were definitely human legs trailing behind it and the torso was built like a human. Because it came from behind, I did not see a face. But, looking back, I'm glad I didn't."

A colleague sent me a report about a March 28, 2002, sighting from Pringle Lake in Calhoun County.

Around 11 a.m., Mark Hakemack and a friend were on an airboat fishing on the northwest side of the lake. The day was hazy and there was some broken cloud cover. The pair had caught several trout and were relaxing and talking when Mark noticed something in the sky.

The two watched as a bird-like creature flew in and out of the clouds. Hakemack said the creature was gray toned in color and had the profile of a raptor. It had a short neck and there were no legs or tail feathers sticking out at the back. The fisherman estimated that the bird had a 10–14-foot wingspan.

The November 2006 edition of *Fate* magazine contains a report about a flying creature sighting that occurred on June 23, 2005.

Max A. Rodenfoe was sitting on his back porch smoking a cigarette at about 2:30 a.m. when he saw something in the sky coming toward him. Peering up at the clear sky, the man first thought the object was some kind of aircraft, but there was no sound coming from it as it approached. His next thought was that it was a remote-controlled glider. He estimated that the object had a fourteen-foot wingspan, and he watched it carefully as it moved through the sky.

When the object was about 100 feet away, Rodenfoe let out an exclamation because he realized the object wasn't a glider at all, but something living. The man's exclamation attracted the flying figure's attention, and it turned its head to look directly at him with what Rodenfoe says were "eagle-like eyes." He also reported that he felt that the eyes were "distinctly predatory, perhaps evaluating his suitability as a meal." The man fled inside his home, retrieved a gun, then went back out on the porch.

Rodenfoe apparently didn't fire at the creature, nor did the thing try to attack him. It soon flew out of sight leaving the man puzzled and disturbed by what he had witnessed.

The witness reports that the creature's body was covered with shiny black fur and that there was an "added fringe of longer hair that made a soft fluttering sound along the edges of the bat-like wings."

Rodenfoe added that the creature's body was about six feet in length and tapered back to a tailless point. The wings ended in "curled digits."

A story on the now defunct *Your True Tales* website recounted a fall 2007 sighting that took place around dusk between the towns of Mansfield and Venus.

The reporting witness and her daughter were traveling on FM 157 on the way to do some shopping when something in the sky to the left of the vehicle caught her attention. She first thought it was a plastic trash bag that had been swept up by the wind, but as the object got closer and descended from the sky, she realized it was something much larger. Her next thought was that it was a person using a glider of some kind, but when it was in clear view, she saw that it was a "human form with wings attached."

The figure never flapped its wings, but glided so close that the women thought it was going to land on top of the vehicle. The windows were partially opened, but they didn't hear any sound from the figure. The driver rolled the windows up and continued without stopping, suddenly concerned about the creature and her and her daughter's safety.

According to the report, the figure "looked dark brown or black, [with the] texture of a toe sack and leather, kind of raggedy and worn-looking. Didn't have feathers…didn't see face. Body of a human and wings were like a bat but not fully extended."

As quickly as it had appeared, the creature was suddenly gone, and once the driver was a couple of miles down the road, she asked her daughter if she had seen the thing. The younger woman had also seen the flying figure and described it the same way as her mother did. The reporting witness said the creature had made her think of something from the movie *Jeepers Creepers*.

On May 12, 2008, a San Antonio resident named Adam Moran spotted a giant bird in the middle of the road. He reports:

"At the intersection of Seneca and Evers, I saw an absolutely enormous bird land in the middle of the road. I was about 50 to 100 yards away, but it resembled a turkey vulture, but much bigger."

Using a van that had stopped ahead of him as a point of reference, Moran estimated that the bird stood at least three feet tall. Moran watched the bird take off from the spot, recounting: "When it took off again, the wings were so enormous that I could see them ripple…if the wings were less than 10 to 12 feet, I'd be shocked" (Gerhard, *Monsters of Texas*).

MUFON received a report about an incident in San Antonio that occurred on the afternoon of April 19, 2009.

The reporting witness was at her home near the San Antonio International Airport. She was talking on her cellphone while walking down the sidewalk. As she turned toward her house, she noticed something in the sky above—a large, black "man-bird." The flying man was coming from the east at a distance of about three blocks. It seemed to glide easily through the air and made no noise as it flew.

Realizing how strange looking the entity was, the woman rushed into her house and called for her husband and son to come outside to see the thing. The pair made it out just in time to see the winged creature before it vanished behind a large cluster of trees.

Writing on his *Texas Cryptid Hunter* blog, Michael Mays posted a November 9, 2010, article about Texas Pterosaurs that received some interesting responses in the comments section, specifically, from people reporting that they had seen the strange creatures themselves. One anonymous writer reports on April 21, 2015:

"My wife and I saw one with about a 5-foot wingspan fly over a remote area west of Blanco, Texas, in 2013. It was off Crabapple Road north of Kendalia. The claws on the wings and the unique head were clearly visible. It was about 60 feet in the air and gliding."

A writer named Eddy Cardenas posted on October 9, 2015, about a 2008 sighting. Cardenas writes:

"My cousin and I saw a creature we could not explain in Midland, TX. We were working out at a local middle school in 2008. As we were jogging, we heard loud thumps in the air above and behind us and looked up to see a large flying creature bigger than any bird I've seen. It had a large, long, pointed beak and appeared tan or brown in color. It was low enough that we could see it didn't look like it had feathers, maybe 30ft above our heads. It was about 6ft long with an 8-12ft wingspan. I believe we saw some rare or undiscovered creature that my cousin and I still call a pterodactyl."

An article from Stephen Wagner on the *Liveabout.com* website reports an account of a prehistoric looking flying creature that appeared in the fall of 2018. The witness, who asked to remain anonymous, lives in a rural area of Texas.

On November 6 at about 10:15 in the morning, the witness went outside, looked up in the sky, and saw a large, flying creature. The woman admits that the creature "probably looked bigger than it was because I was excited and even a little bit scared." Despite her excitement, the woman took a good look at the odd beast. She reported that it had a long, sharp beak, and a very long tail. "The thing looked to be a little bit bigger than a private plane," she noted, adding that the body was very streamlined.

As for the wing shape, she reported: "It was a lot like a bat, but a lot more rounded on the front edge and more muscular-looking instead of almost fragile-looking like a bat's [wings] are."

The creature flew silently and for the most part, seemed to glide, flapping its wings only a few times while the witness had it in sight. She also added that the thing had very short legs with "some wicked-looking claws" that hung beneath the body as it flew.

How do we explain these strange, giant bird sightings? Some wildlife experts have speculated that people reporting these winged giants are actually spotting an exotic, out of place bird—the jabiru in particular has been named as one of the top candidates to explain some sightings.

The jabiru is a stork native to Central and South America and is the tallest flying bird found in those regions. Full grown male jabirus can reach a height of five feet and their wingspans are over nine feet. They're second only to the Andean condor in wingspan and they have long beaks that reach over thirteen inches in length. The beaks have a slight upturn and end with a sharp point. The bird's heads and upper necks are black in color and featherless.

Jabirus have turned up in the Rio Grande Valley on occasion, and they would certainly be an unusual sight for anyone unfamiliar with the species. They could be responsible for at least some of the reported big bird sightings in the region, but there's a problem with using them as a blanket explanation—jabirus don't attack people.

Beyond the big birds, there are the other, even weirder accounts that have cropped up in the Lone Star State. As we have seen, numerous people have reported seeing winged humanoids that certainly don't come close to looking like any kind of bird species.

And what about the accounts of prehistoric flying beasts? Could there really be some remnant from another age out there somewhere, or are people catching a glimpse of another time?

Whatever the case, it seems that there are a bevy of flying anomalies that like to spend time in the skies of Texas.

The Rio Grande River

PART FOUR
Strange Beasts and Curious Legends

LONE STAR STATE MONSTERS by David Weatherly

Miscellaneous Monstrous Things

Sometimes, strange creatures are reported that just don't fit easily into any particular classification. Sometimes they bear similarities to other reported cryptids, but on other occasions, they are truly bizarre, seemingly one-of-a-kind things that have come from…somewhere.

Here are a handful of weird entities that have been reported in the Lone Star State.

A man out for a quiet day of fishing on the Nueces River had a startling encounter with a weird creature.

The man was in Swinney Switch in Live Oak County one afternoon in 1958. His peaceful day took a strange turn when something grabbed his hook and took off downstream. Most of the line had played out before the fisherman was able to turn it around. At that point, whatever had the line turned and started moving upstream. The fisherman continued fighting with the line and, as he watched, the thing on the other end of the line climbed out of the water and onto a sandbar across the river from his position.

The creature was covered with both feathers and fur. It took the hook out of its mouth, then climbed a nearby tree.

The fisherman grabbed his sidearm out of his tackle box and prepared to open fire on the bizarre thing but just as the man took aim, the beast took to the air and flew away (Clark and Coleman, *Creatures from the Goblin World*).

An account posted on February 29, 2008, on the UFO Casebook Forum, was reported by Lance Oliver, founder of the Denton Area Paranormal Society.

The incident involved two investigators with the organization, listed under the pseudonyms "Bob and Todd."

The two men had a strange experience in the early morning hours of January 21, 2008. According to the account, after catching a late movie, Bob dropped off his friend Todd and headed home. Trying to save on gas, Bob decided to take a short cut on a lonely country backroad. Bob was driving east on Copper Canyon Road at about 2 a.m. Bob crossed over a railroad track and came to a sharp bend in the road. At that point, something stepped out from behind a tree on Bob's left. He hit the brakes and stared at a weird creature illuminated in his headlights. He later described the thing as thin, gaunt, and hairless with long arms and long legs. The report states:

"Less than 20 feet away, this weird, 5 foot tall, slumped forward, long fingered entity darted smoothly across the road, alarmingly in 2 seconds flat! However, the real shocker came when it stopped under the yellow light of a streetlamp looming overhead, then turned, glancing in his direction. Like the eyes of a cat, yellow light reflected back at Bob as he tried fighting off the fear of the unknown."

The creature continued its quick and silent movement in "sliding strides" as it moved to the right, squeezing through the partially open gate of a driveway. The thing continued moving and vanished into the woods on the far side of a field to the southeast.

Bob was in a state of shock and barely remembered his drive home. He closed and locked the door. Days after his experience, he finally told his friend Todd about what he had seen.

MUFON (Mutual UFO Network) received a strange report from Arlington, Tarrant County, about a strange roadside sighting that occurred on August 3, 2015.

At 8 p.m., the witness was driving behind another car when the vehicle ahead suddenly swerved. The witness became cautious and soon saw the source of the driver's erratic behavior—a strange creature that was in the road ahead—one that caused the witness to swerve his vehicle as well.

The thing was around eight feet in height and covered with short, black hair. The creature's arms were longer than normal, and it was very thin. The rear legs resembled those of a horse.

The witness said that the creature appeared to be waving as it moved across the road and jumped over a large ditch. It moved very quickly and vanished once it was on the other side of the ditch.

The witness, who lived only a mile from the location of the sighting, returned to the site the next day and searched the area but found no evidence or signs of the weird creature.

The Bad Thing

In the 1500s, a Spanish conquistador named Cabeza de Vaca explored portions of America, recording many of his experiences in a text later published in 1542 under the title *Adventures in the Unknown Interior of America*.

While exploring in the Ozark mountains, Cabeza encountered a tribe of native Americans called the Avavares, a tribe historians believe were likely Caddoan. The natives told de Vaca about a bearded stranger that came to their home, a "little man" who the people called Mala Cosa, or "Bad Thing."

The figure appeared in a blurry haze as if he were not completely a part of this reality and he carried a lantern or wand that emitted a blinding light. When the figure waved this light in front of people, it caused them to collapse either from fright or by some other unknown force. Reportedly, the wandering entity's presence was often followed by the discovery of dead bodies—animal and human alike.

Tales imply that the bodies appeared to have been operated on. Organs were sometimes removed and the bodies stitched back together as if surgery had been performed.

Some natives showed the conquistadors scars or disfigurations and said they had been inflicted in the night by the stranger.

The entity was also said to show up at tribal celebrations, lurking in the shadows and watching the festivities but never taking part in the feasts that were available for all to share.

The strange visitor never engaged in conversations either. According to de Vaca: "They asked him where he came from and where his home was. He pointed to a crevice in the ground and said his home was there below."

For the Spanish, the statement likely confirmed their suspicions that the entity was some nefarious creature from some hellish pit. This belief was likely put to use during their work to convert the native peoples to the Christian faith.

Ottine Swamp Thing

Located along the San Marcos River and within the confines of Palmetto State Park, the Ottine Swamp is an otherworldly place. Sitting on the edge of the South Texas Plain and not far from Hill Country, the swamp has a compelling and rich diversity of plant and animal life, and just maybe a monster.

Known simply as "The Thing" or the "Ottine Swamp Thing," the creature is the stuff of legend. Rarely seen but often heard, the monster represents the primordial mystery of places like Ottine Swamp in a truly cryptic fashion.

Author William Syers wrote about the creature in his book, *Ghost Stories of Texas*. Syers spoke with an authority on the topic, a longtime resident of the Gonzales area named Berthold Jackson.

Jackson told Syers that he had encountered the swamp monster himself on a number of occasions and said that he'd often heard the creature at night:

"I've heard just about every animal's cry; this one is somewhere between human and animal—like nothing you've ever heard in your life."

Jackson said he'd chased after the monster, plunging into the dark swamp heading toward the sound the beast had made, but the thing was tricky. Jackson said, "It moved too fast. We heard it dead ahead, then all at once, a quarter mile north."

Jackson said he'd also made attempts to focus spotlights on the creature, hoping to get a good view of the thing in order to determine exactly what it is, but again, the beast was too elusive, and Jackson was never able to see it clearly. Still, the man speculates that it may be something akin to a large ape.

The theory is as good as any other when it comes to the

swamp monster. Some witnesses have at least seen something of a form, often black or gray, seemingly covered with hair. It stands anywhere from four to eight feet in height, and it moves at incredible speed.

For some, the most disturbing ability the creature exhibits is its uncanny talent to melt into its surroundings, vanishing in the depths of the swamp with ease, almost as if it can turn invisible at will. One story the man told Syers illustrates this ability:

"Jackson and his friend Johnny Boehm, of Gonzales, were hunting for rabbits in the swamp one evening about 50 yards apart, when they heard something very large move between them, snapping the brush. But, when the two men shone their flashlights on the spot, expecting to see the source of all the commotion, they were both mystified. There was absolutely nothing there, although they both could certainly hear it moving around."

One well-known local tale about the creature involves a pair of hunters named Wayne Hodges and Brewster Short.

The two men were out hunting in the swamp with some dogs one night. The animals caught a scent and took off on the trail of something. The hunters followed on a long trek of over two miles, finally ending up at the base of Lookout Hill near Palmetto State Park.

Ready to call it a night, the hunters started calling the dogs in. Hodges had one in the back of the car and was sitting with it while Short called the other animals. Hodges's dog suddenly bristled up and started howling, alerted by something outside. Just as the dog went off, something rose up at the back of the car. Hodges looked back and saw a massive gray figure behind the vehicle. The thing was so frightening that the two hunters abandoned the site, leaving the dogs behind to fend for themselves.

In the ensuing years, there have been plenty of other reports from the area and Lookout Hill has long been a hotspot for encounters with the creature. The hill serves as a lover's parking spot, but plenty of couples have had their romantic interludes disrupted by something coming out of the darkness and shaking the vehicle.

Locals in the region talk about the creature and there have been stories of it causing trouble at nearby homes. Jackson heard from a man who said that something had shaken his mobile home one night.

Other locals report hearing the chilling cry screaming out in the night and the creature has been accused of ripping items off of clotheslines.

So, what exactly is the creature? Some have drawn comparisons to Bigfoot or possibly the Skunk Ape, and they are good guesses. But in some ways, simply calling the Ottine monster a Bigfoot seems almost too simple when considering some of the weird accounts.

It should be noted that Berthold Jackson, who probably put more time into studying the monster than anyone else, wasn't a simple man either. A consummate outdoorsman, Jackson spent a lot of time deep in the swamp, but he also graduated from Texas A & M University with a degree in engineering. He reports finding footprints left by the creature, footprints that he describes as: "like a small woman's hand except it comes to a point at the base of the palm."

To their credit, Palmetto State Park isn't shy about their swamp monster, something that becomes clear when visiting the park's gift shop. Inside, you'll find swamp monster t-shirts and hats for sale. On the wall is a framed photo taken by a camper in 2011. The photo is allegedly of the mysterious swamp monster. If true, it's an incredible catch, considering the thing's ability to become virtually invisible.

Sea monsters may lurk off the coast of Texas

Water Monsters

There's plenty of water in Texas but for the state's size, historic accounts of water monsters are somewhat slim.

Lake Granbury is purportedly home to a giant serpent-like creature that has lived in the waters since early Spanish settlers first came to the area. The creature is known as "One Eye," though there's little detail to explain the moniker. Some researchers believe the creature is, or was, a species of giant eel.

Lake Weatherford is also purportedly the lair of a water monster, one that's said to be a "man-eating, devil-water-cow." As intriguing as this monster sounds, there are sadly no stories to give us any detail about the supposed creature.

The May 17, 1872, edition of the *Galveston Daily News* reported that a sea serpent had been spotted off the coast on May 13 that year. Captain A. Hassell of the Norwegian ship *St. Olaf* recorded the encounter in his ship's log, noting that the creature was at least one hundred feet in length with a width of not less than six feet. The creature had three or four fins and resembled a land snake.

The creature was on the surface of the water and moved in a serpentine manner, lifting its head up as it did so. The ship was about two hundred feet from the serpent, giving the entire crew a good view.

The sea serpent was yellow green in color and had brown spots on the upper portion of its body. The underbelly was white. The men watched the creature for ten minutes before it swam away out of sight.

An October 26, 1899, item in the *Dallas Morning News* detailed a sea serpent sighting in the gulf reported by Captain Gus Christiansen of the tug *Charles Clarke*.

The tug was on its way to Horn Island when it passed within forty feet of an unusual creature. The captain said the creature was "apparently about seventy-five feet long. Long fins protruded from the surface of the water…it had flippers on the side with which it propelled itself."

The captain noted that the sea at the time was completely calm and "resembled a sea of glass."

One Captain Carrol also chimed in that he had seen a serpent in the water near Galveston the previous summer. Carrol said that the "horrible thing" was "the queerest looking thing I ever saw. It had its mouth open and was as big as an apple barrel. It appeared to be all head. From the back of the head was a sort of long horn or tail as big around as that iron post supporting the awning, and the body was covered with green hair."

The June 30, 1908, edition of the *New York Times* noted that Captain G.A. Olsen of the steamship *Livingstone*, along with four of his crewmen, had spotted a sea monster as they were traveling from Galveston to Frontera, Mexico.

The creature appeared sixty feet off the ship's port bow and the men watched it for about fifteen minutes. The *Times* reports:

"It was apparently sleeping, and was not less than two hundred feet long, of about the diameter of a flour-barrel in the center of the body but was not as round. The head was about six feet long by three feet at the widest part. The color was dark brown and near its tail were rings or circles that appeared larger in circumference than the body at that point. As it swam away the tail was erected, and a rattling noise as loud as that made by a Gatling-gun in action startled the watchers on the Livingstone."

Sometimes the reports are very vague. Take for instance the note in the August 21, 1910, edition of the *Galveston Daily News* that stated:

"A monster unknown by name in the fish world was caught up on the jetties yesterday, and will be on exhibition to-day at the Electric Park."

The unknown creature must not have been very impressive because no follow-up reports were provided.

Texas Folk and Folklore (Volume XXVI) has the following entry about a curious water creature:

"Along the New Mexican border is related a story of an enormous and extremely ferocious animal that formerly inhabited one of the salt lakes in Andrews County, Texas. It was an amphibious animal 'resembling a great water-dog' and was said to feed almost exclusively on ducks and other waterfowl. It was said to make a terrific noise as it plowed its way through the water in the early morning, causing the ducks to arise in great flocks from the surface of the lake. It even put to hurried flight parties of gunners who became frightened at its ferocious appearance. A description of the animal given in a copy of a small plains newspaper of twenty-five years ago (unfortunately since lost) reminded me of one of the greatest prehistoric animals. The great water-dog has not been reported in recent years."

Scattered reports claim that odd creatures lurked in the Brazos River in the 1800s. A note in the May 23, 1853, edition of the *Burlington Free Press* out of Burlington, Vermont, noted that "an 18-foot-long serpentine animal with an alligator-like head was seen in 1853" swimming in the Brazos.

I have to wonder if this was actually a sighting of an alligator gar. While they're not known to reach eighteen feet in length, they are strange-looking fish and may be behind this account.

Loren Coleman notes in *Mysterious America* that giant catfish have been spotted in Lake O' the Pines near the town of Jefferson in Marion County, and in modern times, reports of giant catfish have come in from other places around the state.

Giant alligators reportedly lurk in Lake Travis in the Central Texas counties of Travis and Burnet. One legend says that a local man once released hundreds of baby alligators into the lake and that the creatures grew to monstrous proportions.

While it's true that alligators have occasionally been fished out of Lake Travis, they are typically small specimens of several feet in length. Wildlife officials state that the animals are likely exotic pets that were released by their owners once they started to grow to unmanageable size.

Lake Travis

Lake Travis is a popular outdoor recreation area that gets a large number of visitors on a regular basis. Camping, fishing, boating, swimming, and scuba diving are a few of the popular activities at the lake so if a horde of giant alligators were snacking on outdoor enthusiasts, we would certainly have more evidence at this point.

Texas has an abundance of snakes

Snakes

There are a wide range of snake species in Texas including nonvenomous snakes such as the western ribbon snake, the coachwhip, the checkered garter snake, the rough greensnake and the gopher snake.

There's no shortage of venomous snakes in the state either. Rattlesnakes include timber, Mojave, blacktail, prairie, and western diamondback. Other venomous species include the copperhead and the cottonmouth.

With so many snakes present, it comes as no surprise that stories of especially large specimens have cropped up over the years.

The western diamondback, the most common rattler found in Texas, easily grows to four feet or more. The longest verified on record was seven feet in length but there are plenty of stories of people claiming to have seen even larger diamondbacks of twelve to fifteen feet.

Such tales aside, there are a few historical big snake accounts that bear looking at here.

A rather strange article from the August 17, 1889, edition of the Davenport, Texas, *Morning Tribune* reports that a Frenchman living in Gainesville, Texas, made a startling discovery. The story, under the headline "It Swallowed the Man," states:

"After reaching a depth of 4 feet, and while in a formation of limestone gravel that had continued almost uninterruptedly from the surface down, Mr. Sommes came upon the vertebra and ribs of an animal. The ribs were about the size of a small pig's and rapidly tapered. Carefully unearthing the bones toward the tapering end, Mr. Sommes came to the rattles, which, when counted, numbered 17, the largest measuring 6 inches across.

Attracted by the strange find, the neighbors gathered in, and the work of unearthing the monster was prosecuted with vigor. After laying bare 19 feet of the remains of the monster of other times, imagine their consternation at finding the entire skeleton of a man of tremendous stature in the stomach of the skeleton of the snake. The remains of the man, and as far as the serpent has been exhumed, are as perfect as when first denuded of the flesh and were doubtless covered by lime and gravel soon after death. Near the bones of the man's right hand is a rude stone hatchet, which a local geologist of some repute reports to be similar to the handiwork of Paleolithic man."

A story in the June 23, 1946, edition of the *Daily Herald* out of Big Springs, Texas, reported that a driver employed by an area lumber company had spotted a large snake on the Wichita Falls-Seymour Highway in Wichita County.

The driver, James H. Hankins, said the serpent was twenty feet in length and ten inches in diameter. Rankins tried to run over the snake, causing it to coil and rear up as high as the cab window of his truck. He was unable to identify the creature but said he was positive it wasn't a rattlesnake.

As intriguing as the tale was, it was soon revealed that a hoax was afoot. According to a story in the *Reporter-News* out of Abilene, (date unknown) the giant serpent that had citizens in Wichita Falls in such a stir was actually a mocked-up snake made of sacks filled with cottonseed, sewed together and painted black. The originators of the hoax turned out to be a group of teenage boys out for some fun. The paper reported:

"The snake hoax was funny to its perpetrators, but hardly a laughing matter to those who were victimized by it. Fortunately, none of the victims died of heart failure, as they might well have.

"Those who were actually exposed to a sight of the snake probably are no more resentful than those who were duped into offering rewards for its capture, said to have reached a total of $5,000, or to the owners of 'snake dogs' which were offered as trackers-down of the putative python."

The paper did not reveal the identities of the boys behind

the hoax but did note that the dummy snake had been destroyed, adding:

"The big snake scare around Wichita Falls is over—unless there are some who persist in believing that the story of the hoax is itself a hoax."

In the fall of 1954, residents of the Fort Worth area became alarmed when it was revealed that "Python Pete" was on the loose.

According to the October 1 story posted by the *Associated Press*, a Dallas man who saw the snake said it was "as big as a stovepipe." The man spotted the serpent in the Trinity River near Fort Worth and alerted officials.

Officers and zoo officials went to the river in search of the snake, but it had already left the scene. In this case, authorities already knew about the snake—it was an 18-foot-long python that had escaped from the zoo two weeks prior.

It was Fifty-nine-year-old David W. Smith who saw the python and called the tip in. Smith wasn't aware of the zoo escape, so he was naturally surprised at seeing the large serpent. Smith reported: "I was standing on the bridge when I spotted this big brown snake, 15 to 20 feet long, and as big as a stove pipe swimming toward a bend in the river. I watched him until he rounded the bend which was about 300 feet away."

Python Pete was recaptured a few days later, turning up a mere 125 feet from his cage on October 4. Oddly, a zookeeper stated that he believed the snake had been there the entire time, leading one to wonder what exactly Smith saw if it wasn't Pete.

Varmints

According to the November 17, 1897, edition of the *Daily News* out of Galveston, TX, something around the northeast town of Henderson in Rusk County was preying on dogs in the area. The paper reported that the creature was "making its living by killing and eating a dog almost every night," and noted that some of the dogs were valuable animals. At least a few people in Henderson had spotted the beast. The *News* reports:

"It has been described by some who claim to have seen it as an animal about two feet in length, a foot high, white legs and head, with a brindle body. So far it has killed about ten dogs and devoured all except the head of at least half of them. Its first appearance in the city was about two weeks ago."

The *Advocate*, out of Victoria, Texas, reported on a "strange wild animal" in its February 4, 1911, edition. The creature was spotted near the settlement of Westfield in late January and locals believed it was looking for food.

The thing turned up near a road camp where the superintendent took some shots at it. The man failed to hit the creature and it fled the area. The man said the creature was about two feet high, ran like a wolf, but carried its head low like a hyena.

Other people in the area saw the animal as well, and many said they were sure it was not a wolf. The *Advocate* reported:

"It has the color of a panther and feeds on dead animals, as last Saturday it was found near a dead cow, upon which signs of its claws and teeth were found."

A group of hunters in Waller County set off after the animal and their trained hunting dogs pursued it all the way to Cypress Creek Bottom where it escaped.

Lockhart's *Post-Register* dubbed a big cat in the area the "Plum Creek Monster" and reported on it twice in the week— May 29 and June 5, 1980, editions.

The creature, actually a pair of them, were preying on livestock in the area, hitting ranches along Plum Creek. Five calves were reported gutted in one case, their stomachs torn open, and their intestines pulled out. The *Post-Register* states:

"Witnesses described the animal as 'built exactly like a hyena,' about 120 pounds, having the long snout of a Doberman, big in the shoulders, low hind quarters, pointed ears, a bobbed tail, and a white V marking on its snout. The larger one apparently had dark brown shaggy fur, while the smaller one (twice as big as a 'cow dog') had lighter brown-gray fur."

Local experts were skeptical of anything out of the ordinary, of course, and stated that the calves were likely killed by coyotes. The paper added that an exotic game farm in the area had purportedly lost some hyenas a few years prior to the attacks.

Varmints

Black Panthers

It's an accepted fact that there are mountain lions in the state of Texas. According to the state's parks and wildlife department, mountain lions are mainly found in the Trans-Pecos and the brushlands of south Texas, as well as portions of Hill County in the central part of the state.

But, like many other states around the country, Texas has a long history of black panther reports.

While officials proclaim that no such animals exist, it hasn't stopped the ongoing and growing catalog of accounts reported by citizens who have seen black panthers. The database of witnesses includes seasoned hunters and outdoorsmen, law enforcement personnel, ranchers and more. If these animals don't exist, why do so many people encounter them?

In April 1931, hunters were on the search for a black panther around San Antonio in Bexar County. A report in the *Tribune* out of Coshocton, Ohio, detailed the April 2nd search that took place in the country between Three Rivers and George West where a black panther had been eluding hunters for several weeks.

According to the paper, the panther had slipped over the border:

"An invasion of that part of the state by panthers from Mexico this year has made panther hunting one of the chief diversions for ranchmen in that section. Three have been killed within the last month, but the ambition of every rancher is to bring in the big cat that has evaded hunters and steadily ravaged cattle herds all over that section."

The *Tribune* also reported that several people in the area had spotted the cat in the early mornings, though the animal was always out of gun range. The panther had been spotted near corrals and ranch houses. Hunters tracking the big cat found a trail littered with the remains of half-devoured colts and yearlings.

A United Press story from September 13, 1946, reported on a black panther that was roaming around the Houston area.

The panther scuffled with a pack of fifteen "cat" dogs that had been employed to hunt it down, snapping the ear off one of the canines. The panther had been cornered in a back yard in the Cloverleaf section of the city and after a brief fight with the dogs, it managed to escape the scene.

The paper notes that officials had initially laughed off reports of a panther loose in the city, but deputies cruising the neighborhood spotted the cat themselves and launched a serious effort to track it down.

A *United Press* story datelined July 27, 1955, announced: "It's Monster Season Again in the Big Thicket."

According to the story, a rancher in the area named Harvey Mecom had reported seeing a "big creature as large as a circus lion" that was flushed out of the brush by some of his neighbors in the Hardin area of Liberty County.

The animal was reportedly as "tall as a small pony," had a long tail, long hair on the front portion of its body and short hair on the back portion. One of Mecom's neighbors had been plowing down stumps with a bulldozer when the animal suddenly appeared, leapt over the dozer barely clearing the man's head, landed and ran a few feet, then slowed down and walked away in a leisurely manner.

Mecom reported that other farmers in the area had spotted the creature as well. When the men ordered their dogs to chase the creature into the thicket, the animals refused and looked frightened of the thing.

Writing in his February 28, 1963, column in the *San Antonio Express*, Dan Klepper reported that he had received reports of a "majestic striped cat" that had been sighted at least four times near Falcon Lake. Two different men saw the cat around San Ygnacio in Zapata County.

Klepper basically poked fun at the sightings, throwing in his disdain for black panther stories along the way. He writes:

"Perhaps our elusive black panthers will cross with the Bengal tiger, and we can start tracking down reports of either black tigers or Bengal panthers.

"I have never heard an explanation of how black panthers got started in Texas. The Bengal tiger is even more preposterous than the panthers, of course, but at least the tiger has a reason for being here...or so the story goes."

Klepper goes on to note that the rumor circulating about the big cat was that a man had attempted to slip across the border from Mexico with a giraffe and several large cats. He was turned back at the bridge, and out of irritation, he set the cats loose, leading, presumably, to one of the cats making its way to the Falcon Lake area.

A black panther was plaguing Haskell County in the summer of 1963. The June 19th edition of Abilene's *Reporter-News* covered the story and noted that county authorities were having additional trouble because some pranksters were calling in fake reports.

Two verified sightings took place a few miles apart. The first occurred on Throckmorton Highway/State Highway 24 eight miles from the town of Haskell. Mr. and Mrs. Bill Arend were driving toward Haskell when a "panther-like animal" crossed the highway in front of their vehicle. The large cat was moving from south to north and went into a pasture on the Jack Chapman property where it disappeared. Mr. Arend reported the incident when he reached town and secured some assistance to hunt the cat down. Hunters investigating the area of the sighting couldn't find any tracks and the pursuit was given up.

A couple of weeks later a caller identified only as "Carter," a used car dealer from Midland, phoned the sheriff's office to report a black panther in a pasture on the west side of the Haskell-Stamford Highway. Carter said the cat was chasing a small herd of cattle.

Carter got out of his vehicle and took a shot at the animal

but missed and the gunfire caused it to run from the area. It was later learned that Carter had also phoned the Stamford Police Department and recounted the same story, adding that he had continued his journey back to Midland after taking his shot at the cat.

Haskell County deputy sheriff Pete Mercer and veteran hunter Pete Callaway took a pack of hunting dogs to the area of Carter's sighting and tried to track the cat, but no prints were found, and the team was unable to track the beast.

Residents of the small village of Direct in Lamar County dealt with a mystery cat in the summer of 1965. Jerome Clark and Loren Coleman reported on the beast in their book *Creatures of the Goblin World* referencing reports from the *Paris News* out of Paris, Texas.

Direct residents were referring to the creature as a "manimal," and reported that it migrated through the area on a yearly basis, showing up in late June and again in October just before deer season.

The creature left behind tracks that resembled a cat's except that the claws showed in the prints rather than being retracted. The prints were reportedly so large that a man could fit both hands inside a singular print.

Tracks indicated that the animal weighed around two hundred pounds and ran on all fours in eight-foot leaps.

Locals also reported that the creature issued strange vocalizations. The cries at first resembled a wildcat but would deepen in tone and take on a quality that sounded like a man in pain. Residents said the disturbing sounds were "guaranteed to raise goose pimples."

Whatever the thing was, it exhibited some curious behavior. A local woman described her encounter with the beast:

"One evening as I was walking around [outside of] the house with a flashlight, I turned the corner of the house, and I must have startled the thing as much as it startled me. It made one tremendous jump and left the yard. I hurried back into the house and called my cousin. We stood at the window and watched it as it crossed a fence and then stood on its hind legs staring back at us. It stood about six feet, two inches tall. Finally, it walked away on all fours" (Clark & Coleman, *Creatures of the Goblin World*).

Despite the creature's ongoing appearances in the area, no one was ever able to catch it.

Columnist Hart Stilwell mentioned a sighting of a pair of black panthers reported by a woman driving on Bootlegger's Lane in Yoakum (San Antonio's *Light* December 6, 1968). Whether this was a mating pair or an adult and a cub wasn't specified.

In 1972, authorities in Corpus Christi, in Nueces County, were attempting to snare a large black cat that was troubling residents of the west end of the city. The city's *Times* newspaper reported in its August 10th edition that police officers had put out live traps in hopes of capturing the creature. Witnesses, including a pair of police officers, said the cat was about five feet in length not counting its tail, and said it looked like a black panther. A wildlife expert in the area said he thought the cat was probably a jaguarundi.

The March 8, 1976, edition of the *Paris News* has a brief mention that a Red River County man named Raymond B. Criss had been hunting a "black catamount" in the region for some time. Criss, a resident of Dimple, said that the cat had killed at least two calves. The man said the cat was definitely black in color and "not buff or gray."

The *Gazette Enterprise* out of Seguin, Texas, ran a brief story in its December 31, 1980, edition on an elusive black panther that had reportedly been prowling the area for years. Under the headline "Big Cat of the Sand Hills? Some Have Seen It," the paper recounted a report from a deer hunter named Edward Woehler, Sr. Woehler was deer hunting in Guadalupe County in November when he spotted the cat through his binoculars. At first, Woehler thought the animal was one of his sister's Dobermans, but the seasoned hunter soon realized that the animal was not a dog. Woehler estimated that the cat was about 2 ½ feet tall and reported:

"It was beautiful. It would run, then crouch down, then get up and run a little farther, then crouch. It appeared to be a cub, not fully grown, but bluish black and sleek with that long slick tail."

The hunter returned to the scene later with his brother-in-law and the two men found tracks measuring four inches in diameter.

The paper also noted other sightings of black panthers in the area, including a report from a woman named Barbara Mueller who said she'd seen a big animal that looked like a "black jaguar" crossing a road in Hickory Forest. Mueller said the cat was about the size of a German shepherd.

Another unnamed couple said they'd seen a solid black cat, about twenty inches at the shoulder, lurking around in their yard and attempting to catch a duck.

The *Advocate* out of Victoria, TX, had a brief note on a black panther in its January 13, 1993, edition. Along with several mountain lion accounts, the paper said that a hunter and his wife had spotted a black panther near the Guadalupe River south of Cuero in DeWitt County. At first, the couple thought the animal was a large black dog, but after looking at it closely through field glasses, they determined that it was a feline.

On March 23, 2007, Tyler, Texas's *KLTV* reported on their website that residents in Dialville, a small, unincorporated community in Cherokee County, were worried about some black panthers roaming their area. The news reported that "One man saw a panther with three cubs, while others reported strange screams and animal kills."

Less than a week later, (March 28, 2007) *KLTV* reported that residents in Raintree Lake, a wooded area near the town of Rhonesboro in Upshur County, had spotted a large black panther in their area. A number of dogs went missing and some livestock was killed, all presumably victims of the marauding big cat.

The following account is from the March 17, 1869, edition of the *Independent Democrat* out of Elyria, Ohio. The story ran under the headline "A Singular Sight," and details a purported battle witnessed by a Texas hunter that year. The location of the supposed encounter is not listed, the only reference being that it took place in "the wilds of Texas." While it is, most likely, a fabrication, or at best, wild exaggeration, it is interesting in the context of the region's folklore and demonstrates the long-standing tradition of black panther stories from the region. It is presented here in its entirety for your entertainment.

"A hunter in the wilds of Texas, who met with many startling adventures, was once witness to a singular battle on the bank of a lonely lagoon in the forest.

"He had killed a black panther at this place—more in self-defense than for game, for he was chasing wild cattle that day—and leaving the carcass, to return by and by for its skin, hurried forward on a trail which he expected would lead to the object of his hunt.

"He came back before night with the trophy of the bull hide, and passed the lagoon where he had encountered and killed his dangerous assailant in the morning. Savage cries and sounds of brutal struggle informed him, before he came to the place, that some deadly battle was going on among the beasts of the forest.

"He soon came in full view of the scene, and a sanguinary one it was.—Four black panthers were ferociously disputing the possession of the carcass of the dead panther with two enormous alligators. The object of the combatants on both sides appeared to be the same, viz., to eat the carcass; and for this both fought with painful tenacity, tugging at the bone of contention by way of seeing how much had been gained.

"The panthers were superior in numbers, two to one; but the alligators had much the thickest armor and could fight with their tails as well as with their heads, so that the battle was pretty nearly equal. One of the reptiles had a panther on his back, plying his flank vigorously with his hind claws, and another was holding him by the fore leg with jaws like a tiger.—When he succeeded in shaking off his savage assailants his foreleg was broken and a slit was made in his side, nearly through the flesh into his entrails.

"Meanwhile the other alligator was making frantic efforts to get the third panther into his mouth. He had nearly succeeded, when with a tremendous swing the huge tail of his fellow-saurian knocked out the panther and wedged itself firmly between his jaws. The teeth snapped together like a pair of copper-mill shears, and one of the tail-thrashing combatants was minus his weapon.

"The fourth panther, which had been viciously busy with teeth and claws at the eyes and throat of the curtailed reptile, now redoubled his attacks, with the aid of two others, in front and rear, and soon disabled him. The third panther, owing to his entrance and exit through his enemy's jaws, was *hors du combat* with a broken back.

"The fight was now between a single alligator and the three remaining cat-savages. One of the three, however, was by this time badly damaged. Some terrific stroke or bite had completely scalped him, and the skin hung down the side of his neck, flapping as he fought. Another, apparently, had a rib or two broken, but did not seem to mind it. The odds in the battle were still not so very great.

"Only the advantage of celerity was vastly on the side of the panther, and when the alligator with much difficulty succeeded in seizing one of them, he was so slow about crushing his prey, and made so much awkward mouthing of it, that he put himself almost at the mercy of his antagonists.

"Still his powerful tail was free, and the cat-like creatures, in springing about to find his vulnerable points, were not so spry but they took some stunning cuffs from this cudgel bludgeon. Besides, during all the combat, the amphibians had been working gradually toward the water, and now the survivor was almost at the edge.

"Once in the lagoon, and his enemies would be powerless. The panthers seemed to be sensible of this, and by an artful movement both succeeded in getting at his throat while his mouth was full. A few seconds of vigorous tugging and tearing at the tenderer flesh made the alligator's death-wounds, and he slid hopelessly into the water.

"Two panthers survived to claim the victory. But they had scarce strength enough left to snuff about the bodies of their slain. Both were much the worse for wear, and the hunter leveled his rifle, and easily brought them down with a single shot apiece, after which he took off their hides and the hides of their companions and made his way back to his ranch.

"In an eventful life of more than ten years subsequently to this in frontier countries, he never saw anything in the shape of a forest jungle fight that could compare with this combat between the panthers and alligators."

Werewolves & Dogmen

In part, werewolf legends were brought to the United States by early European settlers, many of whom were aware of long-standing werewolf tales from their home countries. Places like France and Germany had age old tales about people who transformed into fearsome wolfmen and terrorized villages and rural communities.

In the United States, some Native American tribes had similar legends of shapeshifting beings, notably, the infamous skinwalkers of the southwest.

In Texas, there's a legend from Kimble County about a Native American shaman who once lived in the area. The shaman reportedly had the ability to shapeshift into a giant, wolf-like creature. He was prone to roam the countryside at night, killing livestock as well as any white settlers he came across during his prowling.

Legend says a creature, known as the "Beast of Bear Creek" was on the vengeance trail, seeking to harm those who had taken his tribe's land and forced them out of the area.

The beast was so well known in the area that an image of it was immortalized in solid rock thanks to a man named N.Q. Patterson.

Patterson served as a county treasurer, county judge and even tombstone carver. Patterson apparently enjoyed carving stone and applied his talent to more than just tombstones. He took to carving figures into the limestone cliffs and bluffs around Bear Creek.

One of the images that Patterson carved was dubbed "The Cleo Face" because it was close to the small town of Cleo. The face is that of a strange creature, part human, part animal in appearance. The thing's nose protrudes, and its lips are curled back to reveal large fangs.

Patterson reportedly lived during the time that the beast was wandering the area, so it's assumed that he was depicting the fearsome creature in the carving, though there doesn't seem to be any record of him confirming this. One wonders if Patterson was just using the story as inspiration for his art, or if he had seen something strange himself.

In modern times, if someone encounters a bipedal, wolf-like beast, it's frequently designated a "dogman."

Regardless of what they're called by researchers, many witnesses wrestle with the fact that they've seen something they believed should only exist in a horror movie—a large, upright wolf man.

More often than not, these encounters are terrifying for those who report them, and many people are reluctant to even admit having seen such creatures. Still, the database seems to grow each year as more and more people report their frightening encounters.

The Converse Werewolf

The most well-known werewolf legend in Texas dates back to the 1800s. Since it has been told and retold for so many years, there are some variations to the tale, but the basics are always the same.

In the 1800s a rancher in Converse, Bexar County, sent his son off on a deer hunting trip. The boy was reportedly frail and preoccupied with books and had no interest in the outdoors. The boy's father was determined to "toughen" the young man up by sending him out into the woods alone.

The boy ended up in a densely wooded area called Skull Crossing and was gone for several hours. To his father's disappointment, the boy returned without having killed any game. The boy had an excuse though—he said he had been stalked through the woods by a werewolf.

The father didn't believe the tale and promptly sent his son back into the woods, telling the boy not to come back until he'd shot some game. The young man pleaded not to go, but his father was adamant, and the boy reluctantly went back into the wild.

Hours passed and the boy did not emerge from the woods. With the sun setting, the father grew concerned that something had happened to the boy and regretted sending the young man out alone. The man gathered some locals to help and a search was launched for the missing boy.

According to the tale, the search party found a massive, hairy creature, eight feet tall and monstrous. The creature resembled a cross between a wolf and a man. Even more disturbing, the creature was crouched down over the body of the rancher's son eating the corpse.

The search party opened fire on the werewolf and the beast fled the scene at a rapid pace. Although the boy's body was left behind, it had been torn to shreds by the massive creature.

Beyond this, there are some variables to the story. By some accounts, the rancher lost his mind after his son's death. By other accounts, he became a recluse, locking himself away until he died. Still other versions report that the man killed himself due to the grief of losing his child.

So, what exactly was the Converse Werewolf? A bear? A Bigfoot? Or was there really some kind of werewolf/dogman prowling the area? Unfortunately, the mystery will remain unsolved, and we're left to wonder if there's any truth to the old legend.

The Converse Werewolf

Solomon's Wolf

Nick Redfern's *Memoirs of a Monster Hunter* has a report about an incident that took place in Orange County in 1933.

The main witness, Solomon, was a teenager at the time of the encounter. Solomon was exploring in the woods with a couple of friends when they had a weird encounter. The trio had stopped and sat down to eat lunch by a stream. They were deep in conversation when they all suddenly stopped talking, overcome with an ominous feeling. Feeling as though they were being watched, the group looked around for the source of the uneasy feeling. They were shocked to see a huge wolf head protruding from the dense undergrowth across the stream.

When the creature realized that it had been spotted, it emerged fully from the undergrowth. It was wolf-like in appearance, but monstrous in proportions, a good ten feet in length with a thick neck, overly elongated jaw, and a hump on the top of its neck. The creature kept the boys in sight and issued a long, continuous, guttural growl.

The powerful animal looked like it was ready to attack, but it did not. According to Solomon, after a few minutes, the creature sat down and began to shake. The creature was suddenly enveloped in a "green fog" that lasted for a moment, then it reared up and stood on its hind legs.

The now bipedal wolf was standing like a man and while Solomon didn't think the creature was going to attack, it did seem that the thing was satisfied with terrifying the boys.

The creature snapped its jaws and snarled while looking at the trio. What had been wolf paws shape-shifted into large, man-like hands athough they were still covered in fur.

After a few moments, the creature turned, stalked back into the dense brush, and vanished. The boys turned as well, back in the direction they had come, and raced back to Solomon's family home.

LONE STAR STATE MONSTERS by David Weatherly

Modern Encounters

A report in the March 1960 edition of *Fate* magazine came from Mrs. Delburt Gregg who reported seeing a "shaggy, wolflike creature clawing at her window screen" one night in July 1958.

The woman was at her home in Greggton, an unincorporated community in Gregg County, and the incident occurred one night while her husband was away on a business trip.

A thunderstorm was building that night so Mrs. Gregg had moved her bed closer to her screened window hoping to catch a cool breeze to break the heat. Just after she fell asleep, she was jolted awake by a scratching sound at her window. She grabbed a flashlight and pointed it outside just in time to see something run away and into a clump of bushes.

Between her flashlight and the lightning that was illuminating the night, the woman caught a glimpse of the creature outside. Peering into her window was a wolf-like beast with large fangs and glowing, "slitted eyes."

Mrs. Greg watched the bushes where the creature had gone, expecting to see it come back out, but she was in for a surprise. She states:

"I watched for the animal to come out of the bushes, but after a short time, instead of a great shaggy wolf running out, the figure of an extremely tall man suddenly parted the thick foliage and walked hurriedly down the road, disappearing in the darkness."

The GCBRO received a report from a witness who saw what looked like a werewolf in Tarrant County in 1967. The incident occurred one evening in the Lake Worth area. The reporting witness says that the creature "looked like a werewolf you see in the movies." The witness spotted the creature between the window and some bushes as it peered into the home. According to the report:

"It was crouched down looking in my grandmother's window. I was outside with my brothers. They were playing in the front yard, and I was watching.

"I froze and tried to get my brother's attention but couldn't talk. When I looked back it was gone. I never liked going back to her house. It always made me scared."

The witness also notes that there was a big drop off near the house that led down to a fish hatchery. The area was heavily wooded and not far from the Lake Worth Dam.

In her book, *Real Wolfmen*, Linda Godfrey mentions a 1985 encounter from the town of Sanger, in Denton County. A man named Chuck wrote to Godfrey to report that his brother had witnessed a strange, bipedal creature near an old iron bridge west of town.

The creature stepped from an area near the bridge out onto the road as the man was passing in his pickup truck. The incident occurred around 1 a.m. and the truck's headlights illuminated the creature, giving the driver a good look. The man described the creature:

"It was covered in light brown fur, stood about five feet tall and was walking on its hind legs. Its face and muzzle were those of a wolf and he said its eyes reflected a yellow-green color.

A witness driving north in Brownfield in Terry County saw a wolf-like creature with a hunched back and legs like a dog on the night of March 28, 1988.

The thing was covered with black hair and had eyes that glowed bright red. When spotted, it was running across the road, and it crossed the pavement in three to four leaps. Once on the other side, it vanished into a cemetery on the east side of the road.

The report also notes that the creature was tall, had arms

like a human, and was very muscular in build (UFOinfo.com).

According to an anonymous report posted on the *Dogman Encounters* website, a witness driving through Brazoria County in 1994 encountered a dogman on a remote road.

According to the account, at 11 p.m. the witness was driving on an unpaved back country road when the vehicle's headlights caught something on the driver's side. The witness did not see the creature running across the road, rather, it was just suddenly there. The driver hit the brakes, looked around, and did not see the creature again. It had vanished as suddenly as it had appeared.

"It was flat, salt-grass prairie with no trees so I should have been able to see it," the witness writes.

According to the report, the creature was a bipedal black wolf with skinny legs and arms that hung low. It was around five feet in height but was bent over. The torso was thick and the hair long across the shoulders and short on the rest of the body. It also had a shaggy tail.

In *Monsters of Texas*, my friend Nick Redfern details a September 1996 encounter reported by a rancher named Walter. Walter's ranch in the town of Paradise in Wise County was a nice quite place for the man to raise his cows until he made a disturbing find one morning. Going out to the field at the back of his property, Walter found one of his most valuable cows dead. The animal had been killed in a vicious manner the previous night. The poor animal had been disemboweled, its throat had been ripped out and both of its back legs were completely gone.

Disturbed and angered, Walter contacted the authorities who came to the scene to investigate. As it turned out, they were no help in the matter at all. Officers suggested that a big cat had perhaps attacked the cow. While they told Walter they would look into the matter, they also pointed out that no crime had been committed so it wasn't really a police issue.

Walter decided to take the matter into his own hands, and he began regular nighttime vigils at his property, sure that the beast would likely return.

With a high-powered rifle in hand complete with a night-scope, Walter started scanning the fields each night for the intruder. Four days into his nightly vigil, Walter caught movement in the field at around 2:00 a.m. Redfern relates what happened next:

"Walter became frozen with fear when he caught sight of a large hairy figure striding across the field. Around seven feet in height, very muscular and dark, it had the body of a man, yet the face, the ears, and the muzzle of what looked like a large German shepherd dog or a wild wolf. Rooted to the spot, Walter didn't even think to fire his gun. Rather, he simply watched, dumbstruck with fear and awe as the beast covered the width of the field very quickly and vanished into the trees that border his large property."

The bizarre kicker to Walter's story came a short time later. Scouting the area where he had seen the beast, Walter discovered a small stone in the grass at the exact spot where the creature had stood. The stone was carved with a face—a monstrous one with large fangs and slits for eyes.

Weird carved stone head found by a werewolf witness

Finding the odd stone led Walter to believe that a group of occult practitioners were behind the creature and that they had somehow summoned it from some nether region, setting it loose in the world to wreak havoc.

An account on the *True Horror Stories of Texas* website comes from a witness who encountered some kind of weird canid in Kerrville in Kerr County in 2000.

The witness was staying with a great-uncle and great-aunt for a week and took regular evening walks with his great-uncle and the man's dachshund.

On one particular evening, the normal walk took a strange turn when everything fell silent around the group. Even the dog froze in place, looking at a particular spot nearby that was close to a streetlight. Turning to look toward the spot the dog was focused on, the witness saw the source of the dog's focus:

"There was a creature loping through there, a dog-like thing about the size of a large Labrador-dachshund hybrid, save that on the creature's neck there was a head the size of a bear's, and the thing was loping up and down and up and down in a way that fitted that kind of build."

The witness adds that the creature was "powerfully built," with stout upper limbs and that it "was no natural thing that made sense."

The terrified witnesses and the dog stood frozen in place for a few moments, then turned and made their way back to the house.

A couple in a south Dallas suburb had a weird encounter in 2004 while they were driving to an apartment at around 1 a.m. Although the area is well populated, at the late hour the streets were mostly deserted.

Right after passing a traffic light next to the highway, the couple spotted a strange creature coming out of a neighborhood. According to the witnesses, the creature was a werewolf-like beast that passed by the vehicle at a distance of about seventy-five yards. The thing crossed the four-lane road in about four steps.

The beast wasn't just a "normal" werewolf, however. It was completely canine in appearance with massive legs. It stood about seven feet tall, and it moved bipedally as it crossed the four-lane. Bizarrely, the witnesses report that the creature had small "T-Rex arms" that hung down like dog legs. The arms appeared completely useless. The head was reportedly somewhat odd as well, though it was reportedly "like a dog's head" and gray to black in color; it had unusual eyes. The report, posted on Lon Strickler's *Phantom and Monsters* blog, states that the creature's eyes were bright yellow and that they glowed even when the car's headlights weren't pointed at the thing.

Even though the creature was in profile to the witnesses, the couple claim they saw the eyes clearly because they were "biocular" like those of a fish.

The road was heavily treed on the right side and once it crossed the four-lane, the creature ran into an open field and soon disappeared from view.

I spoke to a man named Jonathan who told me that he'd had a creepy experience with a werewolf in the summer of 2009 while vacationing in Texas.

The incident occurred outside the town of Wimberley in Hays County at around six o'clock in the afternoon. Jonathan, an avid birder, was visiting the area and had gotten permission to be on private property through a "friend of a friend" connection. Oddly, the property owner had told Jonathan to "come back in the house well before dark."

Jonathan jokingly asked if there was something he should be worried about, and the property owner paused as if considering his reply. After a moment, he said that there were "critters out there you don't want to run into after dark." The man walked away and left Jonathan to his search for birds.

After a couple of hours and spotting several different species, Jonathan sat down by a tree and pulled out a sandwich that he had taken to the field with him. As he sat eating and looking around the area, an odd feeling came over him and the hair on the back of his neck went up.

Jonathan looked around the area and spotted some

movement at a cluster of trees not far away. As he watched, something peered out from behind the tree, looking in his direction. At first, Jonathan thought it was a man, at least it stood as tall as a man.

Jonathan slowly put down his sandwich and picked up his binoculars. Putting them to his eyes, he looked directly at something he said was "nightmarish."

"I can't say it any other way—it was a wolfman. A man-sized, wolf monster standing on two legs. It had large, pointed ears, lots of wild fur all over its head and face and big teeth. It was looking directly at me, and it opened it's mouth slow so I got a good look at the teeth. I swear to God, I thought I was going to pee my pants."

Jonathan says he felt too terrified to move. He didn't want to put the glasses down because he was afraid of taking his eyes off the thing lest it come rushing at him. He was more disturbed when the creature slowly moved back behind the tree and out of sight. Jonathan now found himself in a quandary. He wanted to get up and run, but he was sure if he did, the thing would chase him down. He slowly stood up, trying to assess what to do next. When he did, the creature again peeked at him from behind the tree.

Jonathan's dilemma was solved when he heard the sound of a vehicle. Glancing quickly in the direction of the noise, Jonathan spotted the property owner heading his way in a pickup truck.

"I've never been more thankful to see an old truck in my life. He pulled up next to me and he had sort of a knowing look. He told me to get in the truck, which I quickly did."

Curiously, Jonathan says the man sat for a moment and looked around. He locked his eyes on the cluster of trees where the wolfman had appeared and stared for a moment. He then looked back at Jonathan and without saying a word, turned the truck around and went back to the house.

Jonathan, who lives in California, says he hasn't returned to Texas since the experience and has no intention of doing so.

A report posted on the *True Horror Stories of Texas* website comes from a woman named Jacqueline who had a disturbing sighting. The woman had been visiting her father in Houston and she was on her way back to her home in Coldspring, in San Jacinto County.

Around ten o'clock in the evening, Jacqueline was driving on FM 222, a route that passes by Lake Livingston Dam. She hit a long stretch of road with thick woods on both sides and only an occasional home. She notes that the area was very dark, and the only illumination was from her vehicle's headlights.

Seeing something moving up ahead, the woman slowed down and observed a "furry creature on all fours" crossing the road. Recounting her sighting on the website, Jacqueline notes that even recalling the thing gave her goosebumps. She reports:

"It stopped just on the other side of my truck, passing a few feet in front of my truck. It was dark grey and black, and it didn't seem to have a face or maybe it just had too much hair. It was too big to be a dog or any animal. I still don't know what it was, all I know is that I drove off speeding away looking back into my rearview mirror hoping it wasn't following me home. I locked up and stayed close to my rifle the whole night. And to this day driving through that stretch of road I hope never to see that creature again."

She also stated: "It looked like the boy from the Jungle Book crossing the road with the hind part of the body higher than the front."

The post was put up June 30, 2018, though Jacqueline does not give the date of her encounter.

I received a brief report from a woman who told me that she and her sister had seen a dogman running along the road in mid-January 2018. The two women were driving near the Big Thicket when the incident occurred. She said the creature was about six feet in height, had a long tail and pointed ears.

The thing ran on two legs along the right-hand side of the road, then suddenly darted across in front of the vehicle, almost causing the driver to wreck.

"I think it wanted us to have an accident," the witness said.

Another account on the *True Horror Stories of Texas* website details a 2018 encounter that took place around the Sam Houston National Forest.

The reporting witness, Ryan P., says he lives on the edge of the forest and that strange things began happening around his property in September 2018. Something grabbed his dog, snatching the animal up and vanishing into the trees without a trace. The man reports that he and his wife went and searched the area where the dog disappeared but could find no trace of the animal or any signs of a struggle.

This of course was disturbing enough, but things would soon become stranger.

Around 4 a.m. one morning, Ryan was sitting on his porch smoking a cigarette. While sitting there, he realized that the forest had gone dead quiet, something that was unnatural even at such an early hour. He picked up a spotlight he had close at hand and started shining it around the property. He wasn't prepared for what he caught in the light. He recounts:

"I came to the biggest tree directly across from my front porch, and next to the tree was the biggest wolf head I have ever seen looking at me from behind the tree. This head had to be about four to four and ½ feet off the ground. This thing had the brightest green eyes I have ever seen. Captivating actually. I just stared, slightly shaking with the light in hand. After a few seconds this thing grabbed the tree with its hand, not paw, but hand, and stood up next to the tree. I was floored! What in the hell am I looking at?"

Ryan says he was shocked and frightened and couldn't move, at least, not until the grey furred creature started to step toward him. The movement of the beast broke the spell and the man rushed back inside his home and woke his wife so that she could come see the creature. The woman knew right away that something was wrong and the pair went to the door to look outside. The couple saw the creature as it dropped down on all fours and walked away into the woods.

Ryan says the creature "looked like a giant, grey werewolf."

He says that encounter changed him and that since the sighting, he is very jumpy and is afraid of the woods at night.

Lon Strickler received a brief report about an upright wolf that showed up near the town of Bastrop in Bastrop County. Strickler posted the May 16, 2019, account to his *Phantoms and Monsters* website.

The reporting witness recounted the sighting that his grandson had conveyed to him. The encounter occurred in a wooded area near the young man's home. He spotted what looked like a wolf chasing something. The man reports:

"He stood there transfixed trying to figure out what he was seeing, when it stood up on its hind legs, suddenly noticing him, then staring back at him before leaving."

The young man fled back inside his home and reported the creature to his parents. The parents dismissed the account, but the reporting witness noted that the boy was not prone to make up stories and was genuinely frightened after the experience.

In 2022 I spoke with a witness and her husband who told me that they had seen a strange creature out in Hill County in 2020. Jan and Mark (pseudonyms by request) told me that they had been haunted by the memory of the creature and that despite trying to rationalize the incident, they couldn't find any logical explanation that gave them any peace. Jan recalls:

"During all the COVID madness, we had taken to driving around on back roads just to be out and to explore. One May afternoon, we were on a backroad somewhere outside of Fredericksburg. We had gotten a bit lost, but we weren't worried, at least not at first. I'm not a nervous person, really, but for some reason and out of nowhere, I almost went into a panic. The sun was going down and I started thinking that we would run out of gas or get stuck in the middle of nowhere. Mark pulled over because I was getting so distraught."

Mark said that he stopped the car and started trying to get a signal on his cellphone so that he could navigate back to town. He was shocked by his wife's behavior and noted that he had never seen her in such a state. He encouraged her to take deep breaths while he quickly tried to get the maps on his phone to open. As the couple sat on the side of the road, things got even weirder.

Marks says that his wife's panic was starting to affect him, and he was glancing quickly from his phone to his wife and to the road. Mark reports:

"I saw something. It stepped out onto the road ahead on the left-hand side, coming out of the trees and right onto the road. I stopped looking around and was staring at my phone, almost afraid to look up because of what I saw. My brain was trying to process the moment. I looked up very slowly, hoping it wasn't there, but it was."

What was standing ahead, the couple report, was a wolf-like creature standing on two legs staring toward their vehicle. Mark believes the thing was about 60 feet from their vehicle. It was dark grey in color, had pointed ears, a long snout, and long arms.

"The arms and legs were long, and it made the torso look funny," Jan adds. Instead of increasing the panic she had been experiencing, Jan says seeing the creature "brought her down," giving her a sudden feeling of dread in the pit of her stomach.

Mark says he did the only thing he could think of doing. He put the car in reverse and floored it, backing up faster than he ever had in his life. Thankfully, he says, the road was straight for a couple of miles, so it wasn't too difficult.

"Thank god no other cars came along," he added. A little way down the road, well away from the creature, Mark stopped, did a U-turn, then continued driving well over the speed limit for several miles, glancing at his phone the whole time waiting for a signal.

The couple finally got their GPS up and drove without stopping, and in silence, until they reached their home.

They reiterated that despite exploring every possible explanation, they have never been able to find a logical way to explain what they saw very clearly that day.

"I know it sounds bonkers," Jan states, "but I'm telling you that what we saw on that road was a werewolf. It wasn't a man in a costume, it wasn't a bear, it wasn't a normal wolf, dog or coyote that was somehow standing on two legs. It was a f*#%ing werewolf, and I'll never feel right about having seen the thing. If those are real, I don't even want to know what else could be out there."

A puzzling addition to this report is that neither Mark nor Jan could tell me where exactly they were when they spotted the creature. Not that they weren't willing to, they've just never been able to pinpoint where it happened or even what road they were on when they saw the creature. They told me they had poured over maps in an effort to narrow it down but to no avail. They were also unable to recall any identifying landmarks along the road that would give any indication of the spot where they had seen the werewolf.

The NADAP (North American Dogman Project) received a report from a man who was traveling home to Austin after a visit to southern California when he spotted a strange creature.

It was June 27, 2020, and the witness was driving on 290

East outside of Fredericksburg. Around 11 p.m., the driver went over a hill and noticed yellow eyeshine off to the right at the bottom of the hill.

The driver slowed his pickup truck down, driving cautiously. The area has a lot of deer and other wildlife, and the driver wanted to be cautious in order to avoid hitting something. The truck's headlights soon revealed that it wasn't a deer or any other normal animal. The witness reports:

"It wasn't a wolf or coyote. It was on all fours and in a crouched, defensive posture about 20 feet off the roadside. It had its head down and its front legs were bent, but it was still taller at the shoulders (3 to 4 feet) than its rear. It had a triangular head with pointed ears and a short tail. It was broad across the shoulders with narrow hips and a long neck."

The creature's coat was heavy and bushy, and it had a short, bushy tail. The legs appeared muscular.

The witness's daughter also saw the creature. She said that she believed the thing was a dogman and that they should keep driving.

The reporting witness also noted that the creature never took its eyes off them as they drove by. It stood its ground and did not retreat into the woods.

On his *Phantoms and Monsters* blog, Lon Strickler posted an account about a 2023 dogman encounter in Waller County. The witness reports that on April 15, around 11:30 p.m., he and a friend encountered an "amber-eyed creature" on Morton Road. He writes:

"We thought it was a large dog till it turned around and stood on two legs and growled at us. Its growl was deep but low, it rattled the entire truck."

The witness, who is 5' 8", says the creature was taller than him and he was positive that it was not a bear.

The driver reversed out of the area and the pair fled the scene, driving back home without stopping. The witnesses were so terrified after the incident that they didn't leave the house for some time. The reporting witness notes: "My buddy's dog wouldn't come near the truck as it kept whimpering around it with its tail between its legs."

The following Monday, the pair did work up the courage to return to the location to investigate. They did not find any tracks but there was a strange smell in the area described as a "perverse stench like something had died mixed with a metallic smell (blood) and urine (ammonia)."

A pair of dogs that had been taken to the scene whimpered nervously.

The witness reports that the encounter changed him dramatically. He now avoids going outside past sundown and doesn't leave the house very early in the morning. He installed security bars on his windows, added spotlights around the entire home, and upgraded his security cameras. The man has also stopped traveling down any country back roads, even during the daytime, and he avoids outings to wooded areas, reporting that after the experience with the creature, he no longer feels safe at all. "I just want to go back to being ignorant about things that go bumping about at night," he adds.

Bear Man

Sometimes, those of us who collect weird stories of cryptid encounters receive reports that are very puzzling and don't fit into any of the "normal" boxes. A singular report of some anomaly is one thing, but when there are several accounts that describe the same unusual creature, it's even more odd. Such is the case with recent accounts from Texas Hill County about a so-called "Bear Man."

In June 2023, I received a report from a woman who saw a strange creature in Dripping Springs, Hays County, in the spring of 2023. The witness says that, at first, she thought perhaps she was seeing a Bigfoot, but she soon realized the creature she was looking at didn't match the well-know cryptid. She writes:

"It was big and standing on two legs like a man, but it was certainly an animal of some kind. The thing is, it wasn't like depictions of Bigfoot on television. This one had shorter arms and it was covered in dark brown fur. The weird thing was the face—it had a snout. Not a long one, but one that did protrude enough to be noticeable. It looked like a bear's snout with that sort of round shape."

The witness told me she was sure the creature wasn't actually a bear, and she watched it walk away "like a man would on two legs."

Whatever the thing was, it may have been traveling around hill country for a few months. Another witness independently told me he'd seen a large humanoid with a "bear's face" tromping around out in Blanco County in May 2023. Jonathan writes:

"I was on private property on May 13th. It was late afternoon, and I was just walking around when I heard something rustling around in some scrub brush. I stopped, fully expecting some kind of animal to run out, maybe a coyote or something, but this thing stood up on two legs. It was about six foot tall, had dark brown fur all over and a bear's face with a short bear snout."

The witness stood in shock as the figure eyed him for a moment, then turned around and walked away. The man was so startled that he continued to stand there for a few seconds before the fullness of the sighting struck him. When he snapped out of it, he turned and jogged back to his truck and left the scene.

One account would be easy to dismiss as mistaken identity, a trick of the light, or something else altogether, but two independent witnesses make it more interesting. The thing is, however, I'm not the only one to receive accounts of such a creature in the area.

My friend Josh Turner, who runs the popular *Paranormal Round Table* show, has also received reports about what appears to be a "bear man."

In his book *Werewolves and the Dogman Phenomenon*:

"I've heard multiple descriptions of this nature coming out of Dripping Springs, Texas, which lies just southwest of Austin. Very recently, I had an eyewitness from Ohio named Jenna Perry on my show. Jenna related to me how she and her husband were visiting Dripping Springs earlier this year 2023—They had rented an Airbnb in a remote wooded area, and one night she awoke around 2:00 a.m., sat up in bed, and saw a massive figure standing just outside the sliding glass doors. Jenna, whose husband stands six feet, eight inches tall, estimated that the subject must have been at least eight feet tall. She locked eyes with the creature and described it as having a very broad head and bearlike features, including a short muzzle."

Jenna told Turner that she felt like the creature was "sinister in nature." Seeing the thing caused her to scream, and by the time her husband investigated, the thing had disappeared.

With such a small number of cases, it's difficult to know exactly what to make of these purported "bear man" sightings. There is of course still a chance that all the witnesses saw an actual bear, or perhaps something unusual such as a Bigfoot that was oddly deformed.

It's curious to note though that there's an old legend in Hill County about a bear man that once caused trouble in the town of Marble Falls in Burnet County.

A report in the *Daily Herald* out of Biloxi, Mississippi, claimed that a girl named Ramie Arland was carried off by a "bear man" in 1901.

According to the story, Ramie's mother was in the house when she heard her daughter screaming outside. Ramie had been out tending to some animals at the time. Mrs. Arland grabbed a gun and rushed out to see what was wrong. As she did, she heard other screams mixed with those coming from her daughter. These were high pitched and sounded like the screams of a mountain lion.

Mrs. Arland searched the area but could find no sign of her daughter, the young woman had vanished. Arland quickly alerted others in the community and an armed search party was organized to search for the missing woman.

The group searched through the night but could find no sign of the young Arland woman. This in itself was puzzling. If the girl had been attacked by a mountain lion, there would certainly have been blood or other traces of the attack.

It seems that Ramie wasn't missing very long, however. A man out hunting several miles from the Arland home found the girl wandering around in the woods. The hunter accompanied Ramie back to the safety of her home.

Once she was back with her family, Ramie shared the strange story of her kidnapping. She recounted that she was walking along a narrow trail when she saw a large black bear. The bear turned and fled when another animal appeared on the scene. This creature ran on all fours. Ramie stated:

"I saw at a glance that the monster in some way resembled a human being and it flashed across my mind that I was being confronted by the 'Bear King' of the Kickapoos. The beast threw one of its long arms about my neck, glared into my eyes, and uttered a horrible sound. I expected to be torn to fragments. The creature seized me and ran toward the mountains."

Ramie claimed that the creature carried her off to a cave and threw her to the ground inside. She tried to escape, but each time she was knocked back down.

Once the girl stopped fighting, the creature calmed down. It then lay down and fell asleep. Ramie waited about an hour to be sure the thing was in a deep slumber, then she slipped out of the cave and made her escape into the woods where she was found by the hunter.

After hearing about the girl's ordeal, locals decided to hunt the bear creature down and kill it before it caused more harm. A group of hunters followed Arland's directions to a cave in the Moon Mountains where they found the creature. News sources detailed the encounter:

"When the settlers and cowboys heard this strange story, they at once set out in the direction of the Moon Mountains for the purpose of destroying the monster. It ground its teeth together, and, while pounding its breast, it would roar and scream like a panther. It was now so apparent to the hunters that the thing was at least human in shape that they hesitated to fire upon it. While they were deliberating, it suddenly bounded with rage straight toward the astounded hunters. They were compelled to kill it in self-defense" (*Daily Herald*, May 19, 1901).

At that point, the story ends so we have no idea what became of the body of this strange bear man or indeed, if there is any truth at all to the tale. On the surface, the story would appear to be a fabrication of creative "news" reports of the day, drawn from an imaginative writer's mind. The reference to the "Moon Mountains" is especially problematic since there's no such mountain range anywhere in the state of Texas.

Popular lore says that the bear creature legend goes far back in the area's history. Purportedly, the Kickapoo claimed that the Bear King was a sort of guardian who protected the tribe from bears in the region.

It is possible, of course, that there's some truth to the story and that it was exaggerated by either the person who related it, or by the writer who provided copy for the papers.

What is interesting is the similarities between the creature in the tale and modern accounts of Bigfoot. The loud, panther-like screams that the creature issued, its long arms, human-like appearance, and the fact that it was covered with hair all harken to modern reports of Bigfoot.

Today, the legend of the Bear King is still told in Marble Falls. There's even a brewery in the town—Bear King Brewing Co.—that used the legend as inspiration for its name and logo—a bear's head. So at least in some form, the legend lives on for now.

Big Bend National Park

Mountain Boomers

For decades, old-timers in West Texas have told tales of prehistoric looking creatures that live in the mountains and remote areas of the state.

Dubbed "Mountain Boomers" due to the loud noises they make, the creatures are said to be bipedal lizards that look like dinosaurs. These monstrous dinosaurs have supposedly been seen feasting on roadkill, or sometimes spotted pursuing native animals across the hills.

For the longest time, the accounts, while compelling, were primarily friend of friend reports. This changed in the 1990s when a man named Jimmy Ward started looking into stories of the Mountain Boomers.

An entry in *Far Out* magazine (Vol 1, No.4) reports that Ward spoke with a family from Connecticut who said they'd seen one of the creatures while they were traveling through Texas on their way to California. The family told Ward that the thing looked like something from the movie *Jurassic Park* and that it was massive. Ward noted that the father was still visibly shaken from having encountered the creature.

The creature stood between five and six feet in height and was reportedly lurking around in the Big Bend National Park. Ward learned about the Mountain Boomer legend and realized it fit with the description of the creature the family had spotted in the area.

Other reports of the creatures began cropping up in the 2000s from various locations around Texas.

A witness from Hebbronville, Jim Hogg County, spotted what looked like a prehistoric beast in April 2011.

The witness, MG, told researcher Lon Strickler that she was

walking to a friend's home when she spotted a trail of dust on the side of the road. As she watched, the thing that was kicking the dust up got closer and soon came into view. She reports:

"About 40 feet in front of me was what I can only describe as a little T-Rex dinosaur, about 2-2 ½ ft in height. It didn't stop running as it dashed across the road into a smaller field. It was light reddish brown, stood on two legs and had a long tail that was straight out as it ran. There is no way that this was a lizard known to live here" (*Phantoms and Monsters* October 9, 2015).

My good friend and colleague the late JC Johnson received several reports of living dinosaurs being spotted in west Texas. One account he related to me came from a young woman who saw one of the creatures while she was on break from college. The woman was an outdoor enthusiast and she and a friend were driving to Big Bend National Park to do some exploring.

It was a spring afternoon in 2012, and the pair were not far from the park when the witness saw a trail of dust just ahead on the passenger side of the vehicle moving parallel to the car. She was puzzled by what was causing the dust to come up and she mentioned it to the driver. He glanced over but said he wasn't sure and that perhaps it was a dust devil. The woman replied that it couldn't be a dust devil because it was a long trail. She thought at first that it was someone in a dune buggy. There was some object at the front of the trail, but she couldn't see it clearly enough to discern what it was.

Whatever it was, it continued moving in the same direction the couple were traveling and it was moving fast enough to outpace their vehicle.

About ten to fifteen minutes later, the woman noticed the dust trail again on her side; this time, it was moving toward the road. In moments, the source of the trail appeared—a creature that looked like a small dinosaur.

The thing ran across the road in front of the vehicle and continued running away on the driver's side of the car. Both the woman and the driver saw the creature. She says it was around three feet in height, had leathery skin that was reddish-brown in color and a long tail that trailed out straight behind it. The thing's head was large, and its mouth was open, displaying large teeth and powerful jaws.

The couple spoke briefly about the creature, but the man didn't want to tell anyone else lest they think he was crazy for reporting what looked to be a living dinosaur.

The woman contacted Johnson with the account sometime after hearing him on *Coast to Coast AM*.

Researcher Lon Strickler received information from a witness in Brooks County about dinosaur sightings there. The October 14, 2013, posting on *Phantoms and Monsters* has the report:

"I live near Falfurrias, TX, which is about 18 miles east of Hebbronville. I and others have seen those creatures. My neighbor and I saw a pair in December 2012 on the roadway behind our houses. We were scared to report our sighting. I know other people in this area have seen the same creatures.

"A family member from Sabinas Hidalgo in Mexico told me that he saw a 'big lizard' the last time he visited us. He saw it while he was driving near McAllen, TX. He described the same thing we have seen. It was 2-3 ft. tall with a large head and long tail. It ran on 2 legs and was very dark in color. The two creatures we saw were dark brown and walking quickly on 2 legs also. It was about 4:30 p.m. and we watched them for about 20 seconds as they moved toward a dead end of the road. We got a very good look."

The witness reports that for several nights afterward, the family heard "short shrills" emanating from the brushy area at the end of the road.

A couple of weeks later, the witness's son reported that while he and his friends were out hunting, they found a lot of quail feathers and deer horns scattered around behind a tree in the area. Around the same time, a neighbor lost a dog, and its remains were never found.

"My husband was alarmed and had a high, heavy duty steel link fence built around the yard so that our grandchildren and pets are safe," the witness reports.

The woman also notes that wildlife officials were contacted about the strange animal remains and missing dog, but the whole thing was attributed to coyotes.

"I have not heard or seen coyotes for a long time," the witness told Strickler. She also added that the family's rottweiler was behaving oddly: "He acts calm and fearless sometimes but hides and whines other times. This always happens at night. I think these creatures are around again."

Some people claim living dinosaurs roam remote parts of Texas

In an October 14, 2013, posting on his *Phantoms and Monsters* blog, researcher Lon Strickler reported on an account from a Hebbronville witness named Michelle Raines. Raines reported:

"My friend actually saw a small dinosaur here in town on a main street! It was evening when she saw it, probably around 8:45 p.m. She was driving and noticed the dinosaur crossing the street! She saw the shape clearly as it passed another car's headlights on the opposite side. She said oddly that the other car didn't seem to notice as the creature passed. She tried to call me, but her phone was out of minutes."

Raines said that the account from her friend had served

as a sort of validation for her since she'd previously had her own encounter with something she could only describe as some kind of dinosaur-like creature. She recalls:

"Just a couple of months before, I had actually heard a creature I could only describe as a dinosaur. I had been asleep, it was night, maybe around 1 or 2 a.m. I had awoken and just at that moment I heard an unfamiliar screech of something running by my window. We have an AC unit in the window, so the window is basically open. I heard its footsteps as it ran by and it was heavy, whatever it was. I could hear it clearly on the ground. As it ran farther away, I could hear it screech again! It was like nothing I've ever heard in my life! It was loud, too, and I wonder if anyone else heard it or saw it. I live in an apartment complex. I just lay there in bed completely bewildered by what I had just heard. I questioned my sanity and if I had heard what I thought I heard. So, when my friend saw the 'dinosaur,' she was excited and wanted to tell me because of what I heard. I'm only sad I didn't get to see it too."

JC Johnson's October 26, 2014, appearance on the show resulted in a man calling in to report his own sighting of a miniature T-Rex in Texas. The caller, Dan, said that he'd encountered one of the things when he was a teenager living outside the town of Midland in Midland County.

Dan didn't provide the date of his encounter, but when he was live on the show, he asked Johnson and host Dave Schrader if the miniature dinosaurs they were discussing had been spotted in West Texas, telling them that he had a story he wanted to share about his own sighting of an unusual creature.

Dan reports that when he was in his early teens, he and his friends enjoyed riding their dirt bikes out into the desert outside of town. On one occasion, the riders came up on a weird, lizard-like creature and took it by surprise. Dan reports:

"I remember seeing this thing and it was probably about two feet high. It stood up on its back legs. It didn't have, like, fingers or like you'd normally see a T-Rex in the movies with three or four fingers. It only had one claw."

Dan says that he believes the sound of the dirt bikes upset

the creature and caused it to run away. He says the thing was a "greenish-yellow" in color, lizard-like in appearance and stood between two and two and a half feet in height.

When the riders first saw the thing, it was on all fours, but as the bikes approached it, it rose up on two legs. Dan reports:

"When it stood up, [I saw that] it had this egg-shaped dome. The only thing I can say is that it did look like a T-Rex, it had an egg-shaped face or head."

The witness also added that the creature had "tiny arms" that were visible when it stood up. "It was angry," Dan adds, "it wasn't happy that me and my friends were riding our dirt bikes in that area."

What exactly are people seeing in these remote areas of Texas? An actual surviving prehistoric animal of some kind? Or is there an unusual, and undocumented lizard that people are mistaking for something even stranger?

It will be interesting to see if more accounts of Mountain Boomers surface in the coming years.

LONE STAR STATE MONSTERS by David Weatherly

Acknowledgements

Special thanks to my friend Nick Redfern for writing the foreword to this volume in my Monsters of America series as well as for his insight on several topics including the Texas chupacabra.

Thanks also to my other Texas cohorts, Lyle Blackburn, Ken Gerhard, and Josh Turner for the invaluable input on this book.

As always, I continue to be grateful for the support and input of all my friends and colleagues as this series continues to progress, including, Loren Coleman, Dr. Jeff Meldrum, John LeMay, Jerry Hestand, Chad Lewis, Kevin Lee Nelson, Joshua P. Warren, and Jay Bachochin.

Thanks to Mister Sam Shearon for yet another fantastic cover for the series, Eddie at SMAK Graphics for layout, and Jerry Hajewski for editing.

Last but not least, thanks to the many witnesses and organizations who have shared their sightings, opinions, and information.

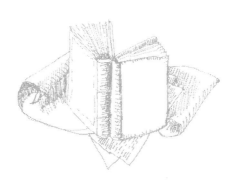

Bibliography

Blackburn, Lyle. Texas Bigfoot: History, Legends, and Modern Encounters in the Lone Star State. LegendScape Publishing, 2022.

Bord, Janet & Bord, Colin. Alien Animals: A Worldwide Investigation—Lake Monsters, Giant Birds & Birdmen, Black dogs, Mystery pumas, Bigfoot. Stackpole Books, Mechanicsburg, PA, 1981.

Bord, Janet & Bord, Colin. Bigfoot Caseboook Updated: Sightings and Encounters from 1818 to 2004. Pine Winds Press, Enumclaw, WA, 2005.

Clark, Jerome & Coleman, Loren. Creatures of the Goblin World. Clark Publishing Company, 1984

Clark, Jerome. Unexplained! Strange Sightings, Incredible Occurrences, and Puzzling Physical Phenomena. Visible Ink Press, Canton, MI, 2012.

Clarke, Sallie Ann. The Lake Worth Monster of Greer Island, Ft. Worth, Texas. Self-published, 1969.

Coleman, Loren. Mysterious America. Faber & Faber Publishing, 1989.

Couch, J. Nathan. Goatman: Flesh or Folklore? J. Nathan Couch publisher, West Bend, WI, 2014.

Crowe, Ray. Bigfoot Behavior Volume 1. CreateSpace Independent Publishing, Scotts Valley, CA, 2015.

Crowe, Ray. Bigfoot Behavior Volume II. CreateSpace Independent Publishing, Scotts Valley, CA, 2015.

Crowe, Ray. Bigfoot Behavior Volume III. CreateSpace Independent Publishing, Scotts Valley, CA, 2015.

de Vaca, Alvar Nunez Cabeza. Adventures in the Unknown Interior of America. Reprint edition via CreateSpace Independent Publishing, 2014.

Dobie, J. Frank. Legends of Texas. Texas Folklore Society, Dallas, TX, 1975.

Domenech, Emmanuel. Missionary Adventures in Texas and Mexico: A Personal Narrative of Six Years' Sojourn in Those Regions. Longman, Brown, Green, Longmans, Roberts. London, England, 1858.

Gerhard, Ken. Big Bird: Modern Sightings of Flying Monsters. CFZ Press, North Devon, England, 2007.

Gerhard, Ken. A Menagerie of Mysterious Beasts. Llewellyn Publications, Woodbury, MN, 2016.

Gerhard, Ken, & Redfern, Nick. Monsters of Texas. CFZ Press, North Devon, England, 2000.

Godfrey, Linda. Real Wolfmen True Encounters in Modern America. Tarcher/Penguin, New York, NY, 2012.

Green, John. Sasquatch the Apes Among Us. Hancock House Publishers, Surrey, British Columbia, 2006.

Mayor, Adrienne. Fossil Legends of the First Americans. Princeton University Press, Princeton, NJ, 2007.

McLean, Jason. Metroplex Monsters: Dallas Demons, Fort Worth Goatmen & Other Terrors of the Trinity River. History Press, Charleston, SC, 2020.

Redfern, Nick. Chupacabra Road Trip: In Search of the Elusive Beast. Llewellyn Publications, Woodbury, MN, 2015.

Redfern, Nick. Memoirs of a Monster Hunter: A Five-Year Journey in Search of the Unknown. Weiser Publishing, Newburyport, MA, 2007.

Redfern, Nick. The NASA Conspiracies: The Truth Behind the Moon Landings, Censored Photos, and the Face on Mars. Weiser Publishing, Newburyport, MA, 2010.

Rife, Philip. Bigfoot Across America. Writers Club Press, Lincoln, NE 2000.

Riggs, Rob. In the Big Thicket: On the Trial of the Wild Man: Exploring Nature's Mysterious Dimension. Paraview Press, New York, NY. 2001.

Syers, William. Ghost Stories of Texas. Texian Press, Waco, TX, 1981.

Treat, Wesley, Shade, Heather, Riggs, Rob. Weird Texas: Your Travel Guide to Texas's Local Legends and Best Kept Secrets. Sterling Publishing, New York City, NY, 2005.

Turner, Josh. Werewolves and the Dogman Phenomenon. Paranormal Round Table publishing, Texas, 2023.

Publications

Bigfoot Co-Op

Far Out Magazine Vol 1, No. 4

Fate Magazine October 1953, July 1979, November 2006

Ohio Skywatcher August 1976

Saga UFO Report March 1977

Texas Folk and Folklore

Websites

BFRO (Bigfoot Field Researchers Organization)

Bigfoot Encounters

GCBRO (Gulf Coast Bigfoot Researchers Organization)

LiveAbout

MUFON (Mutual UFO Network)

NADAP (North American Dogman Project)

Oregon Bigfoot

Paranormal About

Phantoms and Monsters

Texas Cryptid Hunter

True Horror Stories of Texas

Woodape.org

Photo Credits

Chupacabra Skull photo courtesy of Nick Redfern.

Goat Man Bridge/Old Alton Bridge photo by Renelibrary. B&W conversion. Creative Commons — Attribution-ShareAlike 3.0 Generic — CC BY-SA 3.0

Navidad River by KenB. B&W conversion. Creative Commons — Attribution-ShareAlike 3.0 Generic — CC BY-SA 3.0

Werewolf Stone photo courtesy of Nick Redfern.

About the Author

David Weatherly

David Weatherly is a renaissance man of the strange and supernatural. He has traveled the world in pursuit of ghosts, cryptids, UFOs, magic, and more. From the specters of dusty castles, to remote, haunted islands, from ancient sites, to modern mysteries, he has journeyed to the most unusual places on the globe seeking the unknown.

David became fascinated with the paranormal at a young age. Ghost stories and accounts of weird creatures and UFOs led him to discover many of his early influences. Writers such as John Keel, Jacques Vallee, Hans Holzer, and others set him on course to spend his life exploring and investigating the unexplained.

Throughout his life, he's also delved into shamanic and magical traditions from around the world, spending time with elders from numerous cultures in Europe, the Americas, Africa, and Asia. He has studied with Taoist masters in China, Tibetan Lamas, and other mystics from the far east. He's picked up knowledge from African and Native American tribal elders and sat around fires with shamans from countless other traditions.

Along his path, David has also gathered a lot of arcane knowledge, studying a range of ancient arts from palmistry, the runes, and other obscure forms of divination, to alchemy and magick. He has studied and taught Qigong and Ninjutsu, as well as various energy related arts. David has also studied stage and performance magic.

His shamanic and magical background has given him a unique perspective in his explorations into the unknown, and he continues to write, travel, and explore, leaving no stone unturned in his quest for the strange and unusual.

David has investigated, and written about, a diverse range of topics, including, Hauntings & Ghosts, Cryptozoology, Ufology, Ancient Mysteries, Shamanism, Magic, and Psychic Phenomena.

David is the founder of the independent media and publishing company, Eerie Lights Publishing.

He has been a featured speaker at conferences around the world and has lectured for countless paranormal and spiritual groups.

He is a frequent guest on *Coast to Coast AM* with George Noory, *Spaced Out Radio* and other radio programs. David has also appeared on numerous television shows including the Travel Channel's *Mysteries of the Outdoors*, History Channel's *UnXplained, Ancient Aliens*, Gaia's *Beyond Belief* and other programs. He was also featured in the highly successful series *On the Trail of UFOs*.

David's books include *Strange Intruders, Eerie Companions*, the *Haunted* series, and the *Monsters of America* series.

Find David online at:

https://eerielights.com/

Made in the USA
Middletown, DE
21 August 2023

37072383R00179